PUBLIC THERAP... BUSES
INFORMATION SPEC...
SOLAR COOK-A-MATS AND OTHER VISIO...

THIRD EDITION, UNABRIDGED

Wallclimbers

Steven M. Johnson

PATENT DEPENDING PRESS / CARMICHAEL, CALIFORNIA

Also by Steven M. Johnson
*What The World Needs Now: A Resource Book For Daydreamers, Frustrated Inventors, Cranks,
Efficiency Experts, Utopians, Gadgeteers, Tinkerers And Just About Everybody Else*
1st, 2nd and 3rd editions

Have Fun Inventing: Learn to Think up Products and Imagine Future Inventions

First edition: St. Martin's Press, 1991
Second edition: Patent Depending Press, 2013
Third edition: Patent Depending Press, 2015

ISBN-13: 978-0615641133
ISBN-10: 061564113X

Library of Congress Control Number: 2015903123
Patent Depending Press, Carmichael, California

www.patentdepending.com

Printed in the United States of America.

Contents

PREFACE TO THE SECOND AND THIRD EDITIONS   4

INTRODUCTION (FIRST EDITION)   8

THE MIDDLE CLASS GOES ON OVERTIME   10

ACCESSORIES WITH A PURPOSE   18

EVERYDAY EFFICIENCY   28

GETTING AROUND, IN A HURRY   38

IT'S A DANGEROUS WORLD OUT THERE   48

SAFE PLACES TO HIDE OUT AND SLEEP   58

THE GREEN COMMUNITY   80

DISTRACTIONS AND DIVERSIONS   96

SERVICES TO MEET NEW NEEDS   110

PRAISE AND CRITICISM   123

THANKS   124

THE AUTHOR   124

Preface to the second and third editions

This third, 2015 edition of *Public Therapy Buses* is the same as the second, 2013 edition except in a format change, and in the display of the images, with some larger and some smaller than in the first two editions.

Public Therapy comes off, 24 years after its initial publication, as a rather dark and pessimistic work, and I am not shy as its author to say so. The comics format may have fooled some–who hoped to find therein some light or silly future predictions–into purchasing the book, yet the book's obsessions with danger, decline, distractions and dumbing down–words that start with the letter "D"–clearly say much, maybe too much, about the author! If I chose to fill the Preface with my own weak understanding of personal issues lurking in my psyche, it would be boring reading, for sure.

It seems useful, instead, to offer a few short pages describing my reason for publishing a second edition, and to discuss the dated, obsolete look of some of my ideas, now that the future I was writing about has already arrived! As predicted in the drawing of a shop offering Instant Book Publishing on page 111, the time has come when the trend toward disintermediation–getting rid of the middleman–has affected the publishing business: You can now self-publish a book at little or no cost. In past years, "vanity publishing" was a pejorative term for paying to have a manuscript published that no "real" publisher would accept. For this edition, I am taking advantage of print-on-demand publishing, bypassing editors, proofreaders, copyreaders, desktop designers and art departments. I have done everything myself.

The original book has been out of print since around 1998, and I possess only a couple of copies of my own that I am reluctant to sell. If I want a new (never sold) copy, I must currently pay over $300! Self-publishing of course involves a high wire act: One must be reasonably competent at many crafts and specialties. Worse, at age 76, errors creep in that I am likely to fail to notice!

Originally, two books were planned as a series depicting possible/plausible/silly future technologies and systems. But the publisher got cold feet about producing a second book, so I was left with boxes full of notes and layouts, with numerous roughly sketched and captioned concepts. Between 1989 and 1992 I sketched out nearly 400 concepts, enough for two books, yet of these, only 191 were published.

For this new edition, doing careful and faithful renderings of those old sketches has been my goal. My idea has been to show only actual concepts and captions from that artistically creative period. Even if, as is now obviously the case, the technologies appear out-of-date compared with products that came later, I have stayed faithful to the early sketches, only redrawing them in a clearer style. Doing my own book, I can include images that the editor of the original work had advised me to exclude! When preparing this edition, I ran short of time needed to redraw nearly 60 additional images that still interest me. But I did decide to include some of them, which I rendered in a sketchier style at the end of four of the chapters, as *Notes and Sketches with Captions, 1990-91*. Overall, the inclusion of nearly 100 unpublished concepts makes for a darker and more quirky book than was originally published.

HUMOR THAT MAKES LESS SENSE TWENTY-FOUR YEARS LATER

In recent forays into online blogging, I've encountered "trolls" who fail to note the date I created a concept, and tell me "hey, it's already been invented." Yes, I agree! Another issue has cropped up: Some of my images depict now-obsolete technologies or refer to now-irrelevant social issues. Smoking inside an office building was banned in California in 1995, but the city of San Luis Obispo banned smoking in indoor places as early as 1990. Today, an image of a Smokers' Enclosure is neither meaningful nor particularly funny.

Smokers' enclosures

PRELIMINARY SKETCHES VS. FINAL ILLUSTRATIONS

Here are examples showing the difference between early sketches and final illustrations. In some cases, earlier images have more vitality, conveying the idea faster.

Preliminary sketch, *Custoday Care.*

Final illustration, *Custoday Care.*

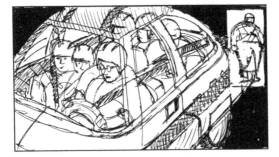

Preliminary sketch, *Inflatable Travel Suits.*

Final illustration, *Inflatable Travel Suits.*

Computer clothing

Instant book publishing

Even less understandable in 2013, especially to a young reader, is an image of a computer mouse "overshoe." The mouse that was available to computer users in 1990 included a rubber ball. Rubbing a shoe on a large "mouse pad" on the floor could have moved images on a computer screen. Now with attached, or unattached Bluetooth laser mice, the mouse-with-ball and mouse pad seem mere historical curiosities.

PROPHETIC IMAGES
At times it is possible to see ahead when one is aware of the inherent potential of existing technologies as they might mesh with cultural needs and fads. Notice how the Radio-controlled Vacuum Cleaner presaged the Roomba by a decade! The Newton-receiving Glasses on page 26 look quite similar to 2013-model Google Glass! This book is full of ideas, many dumb, some prophetic!

THEMES IN THIS BOOK
By 1990, the America I had known as a child growing up in Berkeley, California, seemed unrecognizable. Back in 1950, you didn't lock your front door. Forty years later, cities were palpably dangerous. In late 1984, Bernard Goetz had shot four African-American boys who were attempting to rob him on a New York City subway. Previously he had been mugged and tossed through a window. In August 1990, yet another war, the First Gulf War, had begun, brought to living rooms in color on wide screen TV.

By 1990, the growing adoption of the Internet

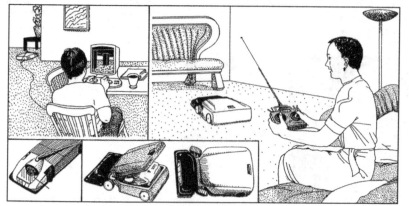
Radio-controlled vacuum cleaner

Newton-receiving glasses

worldwide made U.S. companies vulnerable to competition from workers who lived far away. Unions, job protections and benefits were collapsing. The gap between rich and poor was widening. No wonder that in January, 1991, futurist and trend consultant Faith Popcorn's book, *The Popcorn Report*, suggested that Americans were turning inward, staying at home, and *cocooning.* Many of my images suggest ed ways to cocoon! The themes in the news in 1990 are echoed in this book:

Maximum Security Retirement

THEME: FIND A TINY SPACE AND HIDE THERE

Hide or confine yourself within a small space and stay there; create spaces, products or systems for concealing yourself; stay underground, out of sight of spy planes; live inside a small box, mail oneself, live inside a tiny home manufactured by a portable toilet company; hide from the boss or talkative workmates; avoid child kidnappers or the IRS; avoid street thugs and gangs; steer clear of large vehicles on the roadway; watch out for falling chunks of ice or airplane engine parts.

THEME: DO-IT-YOURSELF

Do-it-yourself, go it alone, avoid the hassle, demystifty a craft, get rid of the middleman. Drive while blind, bump other cars at 80 mph without caring; design your home, model it in clay.

Street escape closets

THEME: WORK HARD AT HAVING FUN

Turn serious chores into opportunities for having a great time. Stay entertained day and night. Work can be fun if the workplace is a video games parlor. Make bridges silly-looking.

THEME: INCOME GAP WIDENS

Plan for job speedup and gutted labor unions, companies having to compete with cheap foreign labor, and the rich get richer.

THEME: NO ONE ELSE CARES FOR YOU

Families are living apart; no one knows his neighbor; you are the only person who cares about you, or your interests.

Dear reader, I hope you enjoy this new-old book!
–Steven M. Johnson, March 2015

Do-It-Yourself plaza

Introduction (First Edition)

Join with me in having fun fantasizing about gadgets, products, and systems that would be in demand as 21st-century Americans try to retrofit their private lives and public systems along lines suitable to the realities of a new mix of ethnic groupings, and new ways of earning a living. This exercise in overheated imaginings hopefully taps into America's tradition of frenetic inventiveness and its ability to re-make itself when problems arise.

I am only one person, a 53-year-old American who tries to think with the uncluttered simplicity of a 12-year-old, and I cannot claim to specialization in any fields other than in Weird Thinking, and Designing by Hunch. So, roll up your inventor's sleeves, gentle readers, and help me out! Don't be thrown off by my dubious futuristic concepts or mildly pessimistic view of things to come. How would you design shelters for thousands of homeless people if the numbers of these people continued to grow? What sports would you offer new generations, if football and baseball have become tired, national spectacles that embody old, meaningless ways of conflict resolution? Any ideas?

Original cover, St. Martin's Press, 1991

Though I do not consider it a happy "use" for America–this great land that is in many ways a place where thousands of years of human hopes are allowed to achieve fruition–I predict that its spirit of egalitarian democracy will temporarily be subject to modification and degradation as technological efficiencies merely serve to accentuate layering of social and economic classes based on individual and ethnic aggressiveness and aptitude. I see that a key factor, access to knowledge and information "highways," will determine an individual's prosperity or destitution. The wealthy and clever, the people with good habits and quick responses, will feel less attached and loyal to America than will the poor, who increasingly lack access to fast-moving world markets and information. Resentment between rich and the poor is likely to build over the years, culminating in some sort of uprising or national crisis.

I predict a tightening up, a hunkering down in America, as the rush to keep ahead leaves individuals with too little time to get to know neighbors or even family and friends. The benefits of joyous, relaxed community life are likely to be virtually unavailable to many Americans for many years, though government groups may impose artificial pooling of individuals to conserve energy or resources.

In the form of a caricature, I have represented most citizens as being selfishly preoccupied, indrawn, in a hurry, needing more sleep, and urgently trying to enhance their personal survival leverage by making use of gadgets and machines. I have tried to make it clear on every page that wacky and weird solutions may be valid, that strange means may be perfectly appropriate to handle strange problems or opportunities. If readers think I have erred in designing the Pushmaster shown on page 62, a product that will only perpetuate the existence of a class of numbed, hapless individuals, I reply that I'm just trying to improve on the shopping cart, clearly a vehicle of choice for thousands of unfortunates in American cities. If you think a telephone built into a shirt collar on pages 26-27 is a stupid idea, I ask you to remember that you saw it first in this book!

I believe that what we call the "future" is a coalescing of the dreams of millions of souls, whose desires at present differ but are wanting fulfillment. A solar cell engineer wants to see the New Age as one in which everyone cuts off from the utility grid, and a smart weapons engineer sees the dawning of a time when weapons will simply attack each other, and the rest of us will applaud all the fireworks and not get hurt. As the rate of invention and information-generation speeds up, there is a parallel march in Nature's production of increasingly clever viruses, world-wide political restructuring, and unprecedented increases in the Earth's "toxic shock" stemming from out-of-control population growth and human "industry." Until all these competing, contradictory trends sort themselves out, future generations must expect to live through interesting times.

–Steven M. Johnson, May 1991

FITNESS WORK STATIONS Corporate support of employee fitness programs, combined with a relaxation of dress codes, leads to the health club office ambiance in the late 90's. Workers tune their bodies while they use Exercycle or treadmill machines that are incorporated into their office furniture.

The middle class goes on overtime

The nation watches warily as the pool of unemployed persons grows. At the same time, there is a shrinking workforce, forcing a single person to work brutally long hours multitasking, doing three jobs formerly done by three different people. He or she has fewer job benefits and lacks the nerve to ask for time off to take a vacation. Sadly, the office becomes the only place that many young people call home. New types of work apparel, office furnishings and employee monitoring systems are created.

WHAT TO WATCH FOR:

❑ Office rest room breaks are tracked and timed, and judged against statistical probability studies for normal bathroom use and behavior.

❑ During the day, the Human Resources Department examines the employee and makes recommendations for possible pairing and mating of employees. The belief is that a married couple would be "wedded" to the job, and that they would make perfect mates.

❑ Roofed cubicles evolve into tiny studio apartments occupying portions of office floors.

COMMUNICATIONS COMMODE An employee who ponders a pending sale all night makes immediate use at first light of the "facilities"–his communications commode. Its sophisticated desktop swivels across his lap, giving him access to a phone, technical magazines or a computer bulletin board.

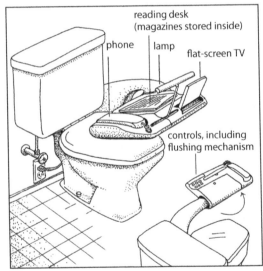

INFORMATION AGE TOILET Information Age toilet systems come in several styles, but all share features in common that include a reading desk, lamp, computer, and phone.

EMPLOYEE MONITORING AND GOADING STATION A multipurpose, personalized working "cockpit" offers employees easy-to-reach services. Buttons on the console operate a reclining bed-chair, a micro-climate control system, a tele-video phone, and access to bill-paying and banking services. From another room, a manager keeps track of the worker's performance.

WORKERLOUNGE STATIONS Certain information-producing offices try to make job conditions more comfortable by installing WorkerLounge Stations. These create an illusion of "vacation living" ambiance, yet work quotas and worker efficiency monitoring prevent any sense of true relaxation.

LOUNGE CHAIR WORKSTATION   In uncertain economic conditions, companies select Lounge Chair Workstations which may be flipped over to serve as an office chair when there are staff reductions. As the office workload increases, the reception room becomes increasingly barren.

DISAPPEARING WORKSTATION   Group meetings, orientation classes, after-hours therapeutic sessions, and exercise classes are accommodated at work in open areas created where "disappearing workstations" are installed. The stations roll over into a four-foot high space beneath the carpeted floor.

OFFICE SLEEPERS Distinctions between work and home life blur as corporations adopt round-the-clock shifts to keep up with global competition. In many industries, workers are asked to sleep inside soundproof spaces under desks or in office sleepers that have a bed, change room, sink, toilet, and closet.

ROOFED TOTAL PRIVACY CUBICLE Studies show that excessive managerial hovering and frequent meetings are counterproductive for sensitive types. Lock the door, shut out the manager, meditate or nap, work when you wish.

YOU NOW LIVE AT THE OFFICE To be globally competitive, compressed work schedules are necessary, which often require employees to stay overnight. The office becomes everyone's apartment, and workmates are seen at any hour with wet hair, toothbrush in a bathrobe pocket, and wearing slippers.

HIDING WORKSTATION Shy workers may be less productive where there is excessive chitchat or background noise. The Hiding Workstation combines features of the office cubicle with the job site portable toilet. This private work space has recirculation air vents, sound-proofing, a urinal and a lockable door.

TWO-STORY CUBICLE Urban real estate is so expensive that businesses install two-story workstations to make more efficient use of floor space. Building codes for allowable room height and handicap accessibility are modified to accommodate these tall cubicles.

CABINET SLEEPER A shallow bed chamber with a fresh air vent is included in these oversized file cabinets. Though they are soundproofed, cabinet nappers may disturb office workers with loud snoring, and office workers may wake up sleepers if they slam drawers harshly. The lock position shows "occupied" or "vacant."

DRAFTING VAN Companies maintain vans designed to help commuting employees make the best use of travel time. Computer and drafting work is possible in sound-deadened, office-like environments.

Stress and overwork

Even as the mania for keeping fit continues to be a major trend among many working Americans, at the same time their work hours are becoming longer, which means there is less time to exercise. Companies often insist that there is virtue in working productively, and for long hours. If you need to work out, it should be done while you put in your time as a knowledge employee, or data worker. If you need to take a long commute to get to work, you should put in your time accomplishing tasks as you travel. If you need to exercise while you commute, you should still understand that you should move your computer mouse and enter data while you pedal your stationary bicycle. Companies, of course, come to understand that if too many employees die while at work, conditions may be unfavorable for health. Companies calculate the cost-benefit ratio of having sick or dying workers when indoor air is recirculated less frequently as a cost-saving measure.

WINDOW BREACH FRESH AIR TUBES Employee illnesses attributed to inhalation of toxic gases from wallboard, furniture glue, carpet formaldehyde, and paint VOCs lead corporations to install Window Breach Fresh Air Tubes. Each employee is offered his or her own personal tube.

WORKHORSE STATION Dubbed the Workhorse Station because of its vaguely equine shape and the worker's sitting position, it offers a slide-out bed-drawer as well as apparel drawers.

VIDEO GAME STYLE WORK STATIONS The generation of employees who in their youth spent dazed afternoons in a devitalizing, dark atmosphere of video game parlours now accepts without complaint a video game arcade work environment. They work in semi-dark.

E (EXERCISE) LINE BUSES AND TRAINS Keeping mind, lungs, heart (and other body parts) in prime shape is understood by employees to be a requirement for continued employment. Many habitually take the E bus or train line, as it offers exercise machines with a reading and laptop stand. Showers are taken in a locker room car.

COMMUTER TRAIN WORK STATIONS Two-level work stations, well-lit and ergonomically designed, greet commuters who use these trains. Modems connected to computer systems of major corporations give riders instant access to their office work task, and provide company personnel departments with a record of the time each employee signs onto a computer. Companies tolerate a little time spent on scanning department store bulletin boards for sales of appliances, shoes or furniture, or on playing computer games.

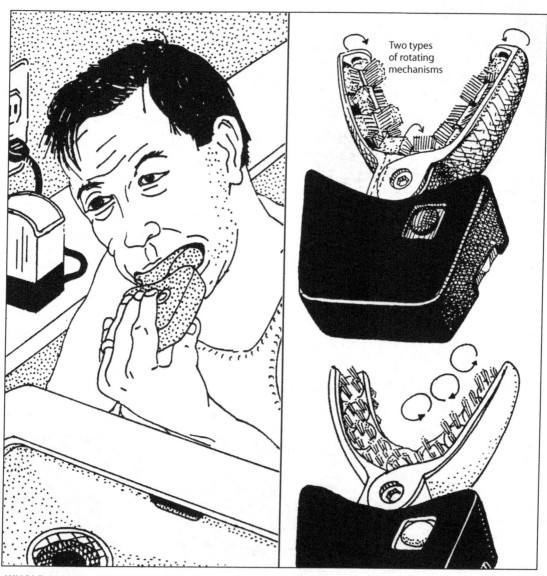

Two types of rotating mechanisms

WHOLE MOUTH DENTAL APPLIANCE This machine brushes all of one's teeth simultaneously, employing one of two brushing mechanism designs. It is kept charged either in a portable or home charging unit. The adjustable arms are fitted to the shape of one's mouth at the dentist's office, and locked with a set screw.

Accessories with a purpose

Burdened by the loss of comforting family, clan, or tribal ties, and often lacking job security, lonely Americans try to "get ahead" using every means available, including an amusing array of "practical apparel" adaptations, and hand-held, or laptop conveniences.

WHAT TO WATCH FOR:

❑ Eyeglasses that enable one to "communicate" with wearers of similar eyeglasses.

❑ Gadgets that detect potential harm from strangers who emit "negative" thoughts.

❑ Shoes that predict the weather with astonishing accuracy.

❑ A suitcase that folds out into a tiny house you can practically live inside in difficult times. Of course, everything is scaled down in size.

❑ A suitcase that is a small, precarious "getaway" vehicle that is guaranteed to start every time.

❑ Underwear that warns of colon cancer and social diseases long before symptoms appear and pajamas with a built-in alarm clock.

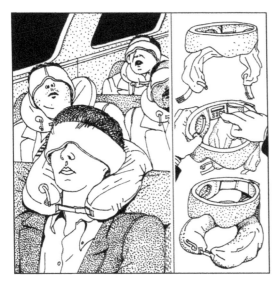

SENSDEP Chronically short of sleep, commuters and travelers put on a Sensdep. This "sense-deprivation aid" is unfolded from a pouch, an alarm and timer is set to play "white noise," radio or cassette music, and the collar is inflated. Users are wary of using the device while in high-crime neighborhoods.

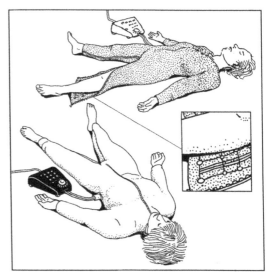

JUMPSTART SUIT Jumpstart Suits "exercise" you by stimulating selected muscle groupings over the entire body. There are suits that balance and free up blockages in the body's "energy meridians."

RECYCLE WEAR Conscientious office workers adopt the habit of wearing sorting smocks with labeled pockets. These may be worn at home and at the office. A reflex habit–aluminum goes in the lower left pocket–is established. The deep pockets are lined with removable, washable plastic liners. A recyclables rain slicker is also available.

BIFURCATING VESTPACK The Bifurcating Vestpack can be separated into its constituent parts if one desires to wear the vest alone, but usually both are worn together. The pack is attached to the vest with lock-snaps.

UNISEX OFFICE WEAR As worker roles increasingly overlap, they erase gender-stereotyped job categories, weakening the need for gender-distinct apparel. Unisex office wear is adopted cautiously and tentatively at select corporate offices. Oddly, men enjoy the opportunity to wear a breezy skirt.

COMPUTER CLOTHING For many workers, computer literacy is a job requirement. Some follow the fashion of wearing floppy disk jackets and suit coats, which store disks in dust-free pouches inside linings. Others don "mouse overshoes" at work so they can supplement keyboard work with foot movements.

PRE-TORN OFFICEWEAR Poverty becomes so prevalent nationally that the phenomenon of citizens wearing shabby and torn clothing becomes common. It becomes so common that it influences the creation and adoption of a Shabby Style of acceptable casual wear. Soon, clothing is sold that includes rends, rips and tears.

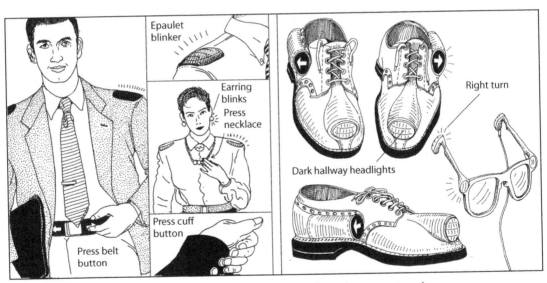

TURN SIGNAL WEAR Several styles of Turn Signal Wear are adopted as a way to reduce office hallway miscues and collisions. The signals are operated by pressing a button on a necklace, cuff or belt. A complex, emergent code of subtle office messaging arises: Alternating left and right signals means "meet for lunch," two right signals says "I like you" and three signals means "we're through." Turn Signal Shoes, which come in men's and women's styles, can be seen from afar and can serve to illuminate a darkened office hallway.

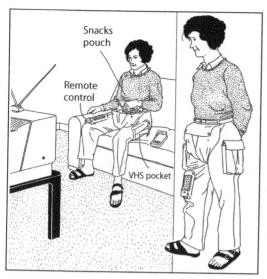

TV-WATCHING PANTS TV-watching Pants are designed with large pockets that match the size specifications of a folded television logbook, a videotape, and most brands of remote controls. The snack pouch's plastic liner is removable for washing out popcorn and drink stains.

MAGAZINE RACK VEST Information greed among professionals leads to anxiety over lack of time to read favorite journals and magazines. A popular item is a vest that holds magazine issues inside a fold-down reading stand for use during boring staff meetings, while standing in line, or in the bathroom.

IDENTI-BOARDS Urban citizens seek ways of making contact with strangers, in a society turned inward. In bigger cities, liquid-crystal Identi-boards, worn like vests, display anything a person wants to sell, or say. Angry opinions, conspiracy theories, or bizarre philosophies are vented on these boards.

PERSONALS T-SHIRTS A brave new generation indulges in unabashed, unashamed self-advertisement, sporting personals T-shirts.

HANDS-FREE TV Designers of small, portable TVs adapt models with 2-inch screens to work inside a hat, vest, or special halter. They are mounted to be viewed at just below eye level, allowing a wearer to keep track of looming sidewalk hazards while simultaneously watching breaking news.

MULTILINGUAL VERBALIZER Melting pot America adopts the Multilingual Verbalizer, that allows anyone to speak to anyone else in spite of a language barrier, within a pre-selected list of languages. Speech is awkward and slow as the computer records, examines syntax, and translates out loud.

HANDWRITERS A noticeable decline in spelling facility, which has been accelerated by computer spell-checking programs, is followed by a parallel drop in knowledge of handwriting, a drop that can be blamed partly on Handwriter machines. The machine-suse voice recognition software and feature various printer heads that are rolled or dragged across a piece of paper (A, B). Another style, (C), requiring no effort, simply prints out memos after an edited version of a dictated message has been sent to "print."

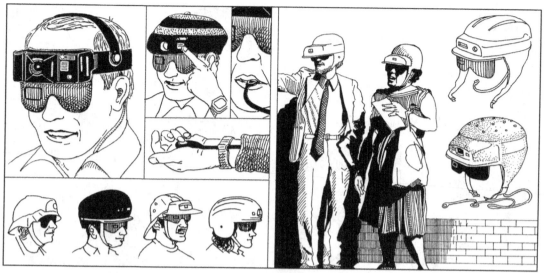

CAMERA HELMETS Auto-focus, auto-rewind 35 mm cameras are fitted inside hats and helmets, with viewfinders built into attached eye wear. The shutter is depressed by touching a button on the forehead or by squeezing a switch held between the teeth or in the palm of the hand. Tourists love these cameras.

HEAD-MOUNTED HANDS-FREE PHONES Hands-free phones are produced in styles adapted to different wearer's needs. The styles, shown here, strap to the wearer's head by different means. Styles A and B employ a stretchable strap, while Styles C and D utilize a clasp made of springy steel.

USEFUL NECKTIES Until the arrival of useful neckties, the century-old traditional man's necktie served no utilitarian purpose. New necktie offerings may include a large rain hat (A), a fully functional phone (B), a phone dialing card (C), a rain hat that unfolds (D), or a personal dictation kit with microphone and speaker and tiny fast-forward and rewind buttons (E).

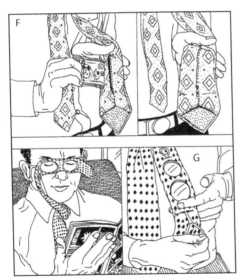

They may also include a secret money-holder (F), or a handy pair of reading glasses (G).

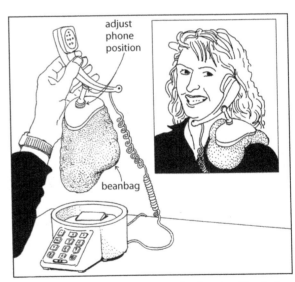

BEANBAG HANDS-FREE PHONE The Beanbag Hands-free Phone effectively solves the need for a phone that can be positioned perfectly on the shoulder, thus sparing the user unnecessary neck strain. The beanbag plops into the well, disconnecting the phone call.

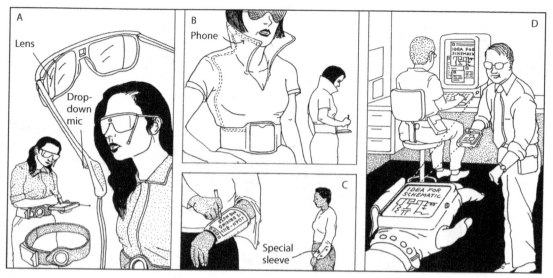

CREATIVE NEW USES FOR THE APPLE NEWTON A breakthrough product, the Apple Newton, becomes the platform for a series of innovations in networking, communications, interactivity, sharing, and clothing styling. New applications: A. Newton-receiving Glasses display a miniature image on the inner surface of the glass, broadcast from a belt-worn Newton; B. Newton Collarphone connects to a Newton that is stylishly integrated into a wide belt in matching leather; C. The Newton Sleeve Writer makes for handy note-jotting; D. Quick Draw Newtons like the Newton Glove share files between nearby users.

NEWTONS IN PERSONAL AND GROUP SITUATIONS E. Newton Necktie is a handy item of work attire with a light-weight screen affixed inside an necktie, connected to a Newton hidden in an underarm holster; F. Restaurant Newtons let diners select menu items, make inquiries or express impatience (that shows on a public display board;) G. Newton Movie Commenters are built into the armrest of each seat, allowing moviegoers to make comments that are seen by all, beneath the screen. Rules against profanity are generally ignored, with the foul and critical remarks becoming more interesting than the movie itself.

NEWTONS AT SCHOOL OR THE LOCAL HANGOUT H. Newton Lecture Tool allows each student to see and save images broadcast by the lecturer on the large screen to a Newton mounted on the chair armrest; I. Newton PicturePhone is either portable, folding into a box, or installed as a fixed appliance. It is both a videophone and a text- and art-sharing device; J. Flirtation Newtons are popular at bars and coffee shops, as they allow opportunities for "breaking the ice" by letting one communicate with a stranger. They are loaned out at the counter, and can be used for summoning a waitperson.

BELT NEWTONS K. Necklace Newtons are worn as attractive pendants. The oval-shaped pendant is the screen for the Newton's hard drive, which is worn in a belt pouch; L. Belt Newtons open out and down to provide a small work and communication surface that is always handy and can be used hands-free.

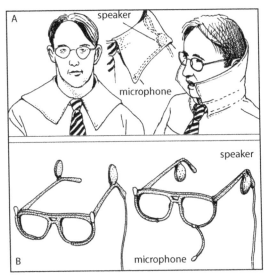

PHONE SHIRT AND PHONE GLASSES Antiquated traditional clothing styles are redesigned for greater utility. Wiring and hardware for phones, removable during clothes washing, are secreted inside large shirt collars (A). Eyeglasses are modified as usable phones (B).

NEWS NOOK The News Nook is for people who feel a stronger desire at breakfast to immerse themselves in news, than in conversation with a house mate. Its "media wall" stores a TV, a newspaper reading rack, a keyboard and a sliding, flat computer screen. If conversation drags, shut out a mate and log on.

Everyday efficiency

Driven by a need to save nanoseconds in a busy day, Americans are suckers for time-saving furniture and appliances, and recreation "facilitators."

WHAT TO WATCH FOR:

❑ Dirty clothes slots in home bedroom walls. Tossed in the proper slot, the item is sent on a conveyor belt to an "intelligent" washing machine that knows the proper wash and dry settings, and the room to which it should be returned.

❑ Home bathroom mirrors that keep a video record of how you looked on other mornings.

❑ A machine that is taught how to spoon-feed each member of the household, memorizing mouth shape and chewing patterns.

❑ Garden robots that do one's yard work and report back findings (aphids on rose bush no. 3).

❑ A machine one gets inside at the beginning and end of the day that assists in unpleasant tasks of dressing and undressing. One model sucks clothes off the body.

❑ A sophisticated phone-answering device that prepares dinner, depending on which numbers are keyed in. Potato, shrimp, red wine is 3-1-9.

INFLATABLE GUEST ROOM   Construction of urban sub studio apartments leads folks to pursue crafty and often elegant ways to add to their living space. Furnishings that pull down from the ceiling or inflate from wall cabinets are common, as are Oriental-style screens that tip flat for use as inflatable guest rooms.

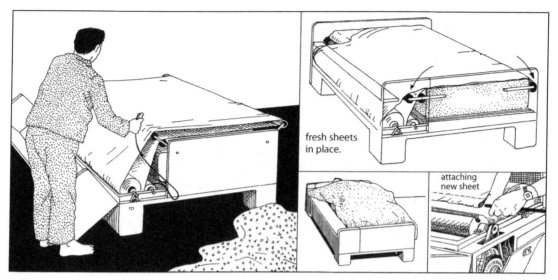

fresh sheets in place.

attaching new sheet

BEDSHEET-ON-A-ROLL The automatic self-making bed, a dream of many adolescents and some adults, is produced. All that is required is periodic forward winding of the take-up sheet roll, which draws a fresh sheet segment around a roller to create a "pair" of clean sheets. The used sheet roll is picked up for cleaning by a mobile laundry service, which leaves behind a fresh roll.

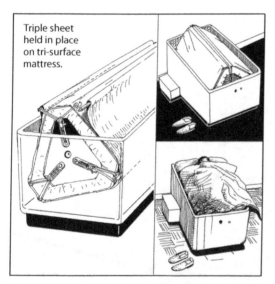

Triple sheet held in place on tri-surface mattress.

TRI-SURFACE MATTRESS AND SHEET SYSTEM Laziness, especially evident among young men, inspires a manufacturer to think up the rotating Tri-surface Mattress and Sheet System. The under sheet is equal in width to three normal sheets and needs to be changed one-third as often.

WALL-TO-WALL SORTING BINS Information overload leaves Americans exasperated and desperate to purchase information-organizing aids like Wall-to-wall Sorting Bins. These convert little-used floor area into a giant "desk" for sorting unread mail, odd news clippings and professional journals.

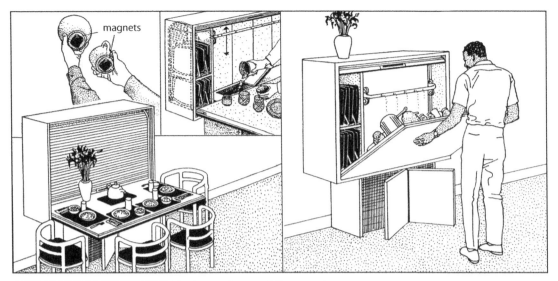

DISH WASHING DINING TABLE Single people especially appreciate dish washing dining systems because they eliminate steps in table setting and after-dinner cleanup. After a meal, dishes and pots, embedded with magnets, are slid off thick place mats and stuck to a metal table that is then tilted into a washing cabinet.

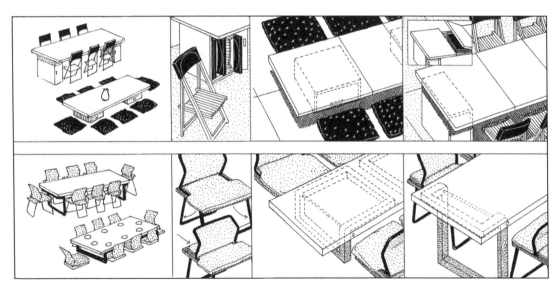

EAST-WEST DINING SETS A chance to participate in a variety of ethnic lifestyle experiences is cherished by those who welcome and embrace an increasingly multicultural America. East-West Dining Sets quickly convert to seating and table heights appropriate for eating either Occidental- or Oriental-style.

INSTANT DINETTE SET   Large families living in small apartments purchase "instant" dinette systems that occupy a small area when not in use. Some tables pull down from the ceiling, while others pop out from inside a wall.

EXECUTIVE WALKER   Hoping to steer a child away from interest in impractical subjects like literature and art, ambitious parents equip their child's playroom or nursery with modern office furniture and equipment.

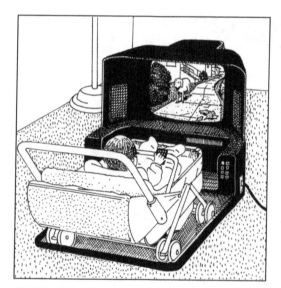

PRAMVIEW   Watching a videotaped stroll on the Pramview may be a child's first exposure to a synthetically experienced event. Pressing a button, the child may replay the time a dog is encountered on the walk or a leaf is examined. The child develops a sense for kinds of time other than "real" time.

ASSISTROLL   Affluent young families purchase Assistroll–motorized prams to spare young mothers unnecessary exertion. The most costly models offer space for mother and child to sit side-by-side while riding along a bicycle lane or sidewalk.

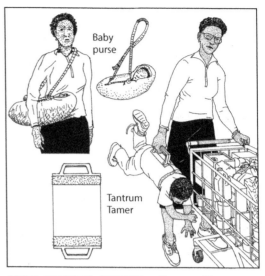

SCREAM CHAMBERS For shoppers with noisy children, supermarkets offer sound-deadening child-isolation chambers attached to shopping carts. These have enclosed seating compartments and provide fresh air ventilation.

CHILD CONTROL DEVICES Tantrum Tamers are velcro-fastened satchels for controlling children who like to wiggle free of parental constraint. Tamers let a parent carry a screaming child around safely, without harming a child's sensitive internal organs. The Baby Purse is a fashionable baby cocoon, worn like a purse.

AUTOMOBILE SNACK CONVEYOR Households have so little time for bonding and closeness that even a moment passing food with an Automobile Snack Conveyor seems special. The conveyor has forward and reverse directions and also can be used for passing notes or maps.

SPORT LAUNDERETTE COUPE Folks with unplanned love liaisons appreciate the Sport Launderette Coupe. It will wash and dry small- and medium-sized loads during a 15-minute commute or errand, though gas economy suffers. The Coupe has a separate hot water system, belts and pulleys, and lint-venting ports.

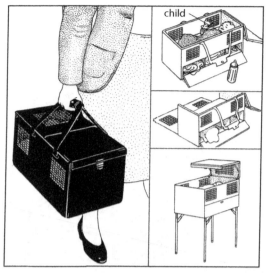

BRIEFSKATE   The multi-purpose Briefskate is pressed into service as an ideal sidewalk transportation device for agile office workers. It is the first step for those wishing to beat rush-hour traffic out of town, and yet it is also a sturdy briefcase for carrying office papers.

INFANT TOTE FOR BUSINESS   Career women and men juggling infant-care duties with demanding roles as executives or sales reps use the leatherette Infant Tote. In black, it matches appointment books and attache cases. A bottom compartment stores diapers, blanket, pacifier, and formula.

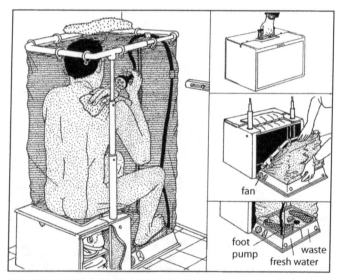

POUCHPANTS   A strange fad develops–the wearing of pants outfitted to contain a purse or wallet in front. Wearers look like human marsupials, or as if they are wearing oddly placed codpieces.

PORTABLE GYM LOCKER WITH SHOWER   After an overly enthusiastic lunchtime walk or a long bike ride to work, an office worker who owns the Portable Gym Locker can enjoy a shower while locked inside a rest room stall. The locker keeps water warm all day in an insulated, fresh water chamber.

IMAGE-RECORDING BATHROOM MIRROR How did I look yesterday, or four months ago? Are my complexion-smoothing vitamins working for me? Should I have kept my earlier haircut style? This useful bathroom mirror answers those questions. Replay, zoom, freeze image are among its features.

EXERTOILET A new type of studio apartment is created that offers compactly organized, small living spaces with multiple-use, overlapping and fold-out furnishings as found in a well-designed motor home. An exercise bicycle, built into a bathroom, faces a combination television-medicine cabinet.

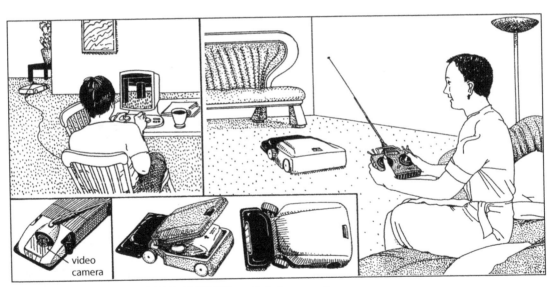

RADIO-CONTROLLED VACUUM CLEANER Robot vacuum cleaners are popular, as are toy-like cleaners that are operated like hobby race cars. Some have video cameras to allow the operator, sitting at a video monitor, to guide the cleaner under a couch or bed in a distant room.

ACTIVE LIFE FRONT DOOR Many buyers choose new home models that include an "active life front door" that's exclusively for residents. Unnoticed by strangers or guests, it connects into a "jogger's bathroom" and an "information-transfer room" (mail sorting bins, fax, phone, and answering machine).

IRONING SEAT In small rooms where multiple tasks are performed, it helps if furnishings can serve several functions. An Ironing Seat is a cushioned television-viewing chair that becomes an ironing board when tipped over. It has cabinets for storing TV program guides and channel changers.

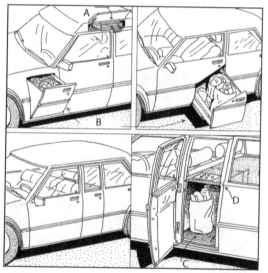

SHOPPING CAR A Shopping Car is designed for serious shoppers, with a filing cabinet for keeping store sales coupons and newspaper ads. Inside the trunk, forming part of a rear panel, is a folding shopping cart. Used on a shopping trip, it minimizes the number of times bags must be lifted.

CAR DRAWERS With parking lot muggings on the rise, there's a need for easily reachable places to jettison packages, briefcases and groceries when one enters a car. Vehicle models offer rooftop briefcase drawers (A), bins for groceries (B), and a hidden conveyor belt (C) with easily reachable controls (D).

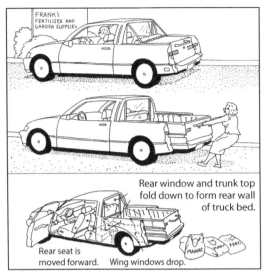

ROAD OFFICE Catch up on work at the roadside or during a traffic tie-up. Two passengers may be seated if a desktop is retracted and seats pulled down (A). Office work is possible with a single passenger, or none, in the rear seat (B). The office is secured beneath a locked, rolled steel safety shutter (C).

PICKUP TRUNK The do-it-yourself ethic that pervades American life supports a need for instantly adaptable products. A Pickup Trunk can be tugged like a drawer to become a truck bed. It is handy for hauling topsoil, manure, or apartment furniture.

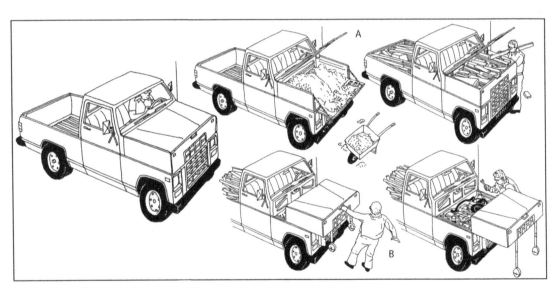

DOUBLE BED PICKUP At times a pickup truck's bed is found to be too small for one's needs. The Double Bed Pickup truck has space for loads in both front and rear compartments. The unusual front bed (A) sits above the engine compartment. Drop-down wheels allow one to slide the front bed forward for engine maintenance and repair (B).

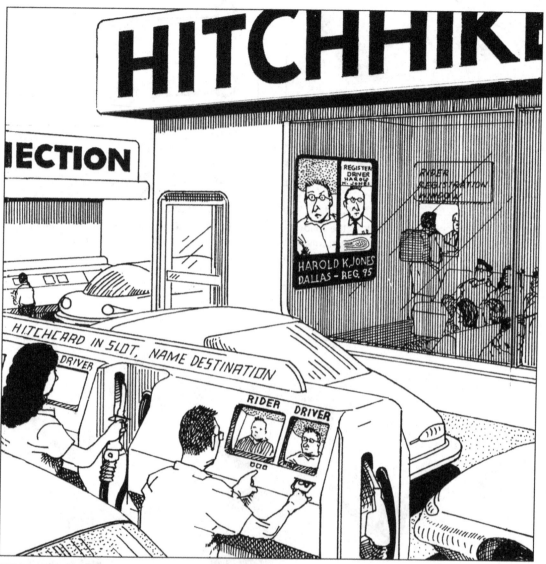

HITCHHIKER CONNECTION NODES Hitchhiking, unsafe for decades, returns to American streets following creation of a National Board of Hitchhikers and Drivers. The Board checks fingerprints and arrest records before issuing cards. Typically, fees are negotiated and identities verified by Identicheck machines at connection nodes.

Getting around, in a hurry

The wasteful, passenger-auto-dominated transportation system is subjected to fine-tinkering and semi-automation before it finally self-destructs. An unprecedented era of experimentation ensues, in which nonstandard road systems and vehicles are tried.

WHAT TO WATCH FOR:

❑ Roadways for blind drivers.

❑ Automated highways. You drive while sound asleep at the wheel, with no ill effects.

❑ Cars sold with a bullet-proofed, "jitney seating" compartment for paying strangers.

❑ Regions where only solar-electric cars are allowed. Workers stay home on overcast days.

❑ Bedrooms you drive to work in.

❑ Dashboard voice recognition systems that learn to respond to "stop," "turn left," "go" and similar commands in case of a seizure, or foot cramp.

❑ Cities with "steal these cars" zones, where cars, one step away from the wrecking yard, are free on a "no guarantee of operational safety" basis.

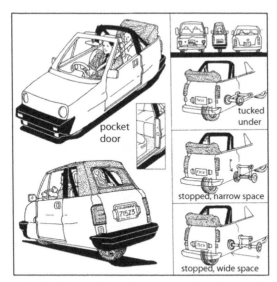

MOTORCYCLE CONVERTIBLE The Motorcycle Convertible is popular with fastidious office workers who dislike feeling air rushing between their legs or don't want dust, oil and gravel on their clothes. If it is stalled between two cars, a set of wheels drops. If there is space, the wheels widen for better stability.

ROADWAYS FOR THE ELDERLY Studies proving that aging drivers often possess dangerously slow reflexes are used to justify building a separate road system for them. Cars using the roads must display lighted panels that report eye wear required (E), slow reflexes) (SR), passes smog (PS) and 37 (mpg).

MAIL ONESELF   The long-awaited day arrives when people are able to mail themselves places. Companies offer overnight service and same day delivery. The attraction is that once the destination address is stuck to the standardized, padded crate, and an adequate supply of snack food and video tapes is stashed, an occupant can simply forget travel worries such as flight arrangements, connections, or unpleasant seat mates. The system requires unique regulations for pressure and temperature control in human baggage areas, and stringent procedures for lifting and dropping the crates.

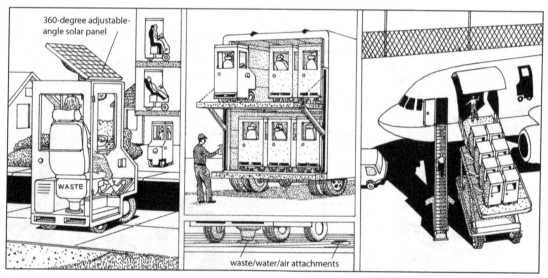

UNI-PERSON TRAVEL MODULE   Some people forgo the purchase of a private automobile in favor of buying or leasing a Uni-Person Travel Module. These fit in modular fashion inside trucks, planes, trains, buses, cabs and cruise ships designed to accommodate them. One drives the Module to position it on the sidewalk in front of the house or apartment and leaves it off upon arrival. The advantage of using the small, battery-electric Module over other travel systems is that one has complete control of privacy, personal space, and climate control. Inside, one may stock up on favorite music, magazines and foods.

SLEEPING TRAIN   Owners of inner-city office buildings and corporate headquarters, fearing a total loss of employees because of excessively long, nerve-wracking commutes to suburban bedroom communities, join together in a program that boldly integrates transit with architecture. Trains for the professional working elite are touted as "office door to front door" rolling motels, with luxury sleeping areas and fine dining. Quit work at 4:30 and literally crawl into bed as soon as the 4:35 pulls up alongside the office.

DUMPRAMPS   Costly, sometimes ludicrous, devices for diverting and re-directing stalled freeway traffic are tried, such as traffic "dumpramps." When signals flash, drivers must slow to 5 mph and prepare to creep down a steeply angled freeway section that drops them onto a local arterial.

TRAFFIC SORTING AND THINNING STATIONS At the outskirts of many cities, ungainly machines alleviate traffic congestion by sorting and thinning the stream of cars. They are mounted on tracks paralleling freeways and lift stalled, wrecked, or slow-moving cars onto shoulder lanes using magnets and padded claws. Auto makers strengthen roof and chassis designs and offer models with rooftop hooks to lessen machine-caused damage. All in all, these stations are neither successful in relieving congestion nor popular with motorists, who dread being caught by them.

AUTOMOBILE ABANDONMENT ZONES Auto abandonment zones are built to accommodate growing numbers of drivers who lose the will to proceed further in bumper-to-bumper, freeway traffic. Drivers may pull off, leave car keys with an Abandonment Officer, and board a nearby train, phone relatives, or calm themselves in "parks."

SNAP-TOGETHER CARS   Ways to herd autos, relieving drivers of control on crowded freeways, are devised. The Snap-Together Car system joins battery-electric autos to a Mother Car to form a connected "transportation organism." Riders may sit in the Mother Car restaurant until the exit is reached.

TRAFFICSCOPE   Becoming stuck in freeway traffic is less annoying when one can see far ahead with the Trafficscope to discover the cause of the tie-up. Using either the earlier periscope style, or the more advanced antenna-mounted camera style, one can choose to relax, or to take the nearest exit.

| Bumper car A is stalled; car B approaches. | B intentionally collides with car A. | A goes into an uncontrolled spin. | A multi-car pileup ensues. |

BUMPER CARS   A major innovation in car design, the Bumper Car allows for playful collisions while in motion, without hurting occupants or car body. Caster-style wheels move omnidirectionally on impact like shopping cart wheels. Drivers commonly crowd or push their way into other lanes, but hate being "wedged." Bumper Car interactions may display aggression–capturing another vehicle or intentionally colliding with it–or cooperative herding as when cars gently push a disabled vehicle out of harm's way.

SKYCAR FLYWAYS Approval of the Skycar concept for commuter travel is hailed by wealthy commuters, who had long dreamed of flying over rush hour traffic. Yet the din and daily crashes of untrained office executives into bushes dotting "flyways" lead to the outlawing of flying cars.

CAR-IN-A-CAR Before all cars are required by law to be powered by electricity only, car-in-a-car models are popular. They have an outer, gasoline-powered car (B), often parked near a freeway on-ramp, which carries and recharges an inner, electric car (A) during trips out of town.

STEAM BATH VAN FOR COMMUTERS Commuter groups form clubs for the purpose of buying steam bath vans, which have showers, toilets, and seating for nine bathers. Water jackets surrounding the van's engine make steam during commutes of 15 minutes or longer, fogging the windows. The vans can also carry light cargo.

STACKING COMPANY CARS Businesses with offices downtown, where land is costly, purchase stacking company cars. A fleet fits in a small parking lot and is operational once all employees have completed a required class in docking, ramp fold-up procedure, door-less entry, and use of safety jacks.

SELF-SHORTENING COUPE In a self-shortening coupe, the driver raises the trunk during tight parking maneuvers by pressing a dashboard button. With the trunk raised, a hidden rear door is accessible for back seat storage of shopping bags. Road handling and gas mileage at freeway speeds are better with the trunk lowered.

PASSENGER CASSETTE   Vehicles with the Passenger Cassette feature offer a useful alternative means of exiting a vehicle. They are designed for use where there is adequate space for egress, as in a Handicap Parking zone. The cassette makes exiting a car easier for elderly or infirm passengers. At the end of the cassette, placed where a passenger door is traditionally located, an alternative exit door is provided. It may be opened in tight parking spaces where the full ejection of the cassette is not possible (see drawing on right).

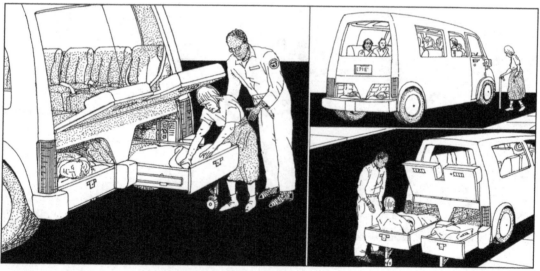

SLEEPY DRAWERS VAN   A person who chooses to travel in a Sleepy Drawers Van must phone ahead and reserve a drawer. Vacancies are rare along routes serving retirement communities. It's popular with exhausted night shift workers, drunkards, and very old people. Some complain that riding above the rear axle makes for disturbed sleep, but most are not so affected. Small luggage and purses fit at the foot of the drawer-bed. The space is climate controlled, and buttons can be pressed in emergencies–sudden sickness, need to use a toilet–at which time, the driver will stop and retrieve the passenger from the drawer-bed.

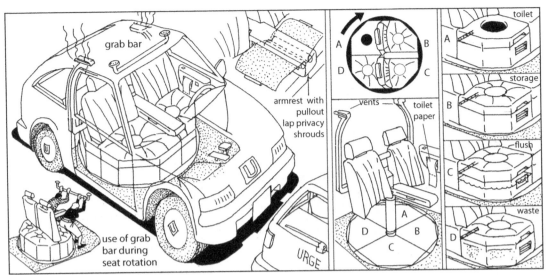

MULTI-CHOICE CAR SEATS WITH TOILET OPTION   Makers of the Urge Coupe chose the name over names like "purge, surge, and urge". Marketed mainly to seniors, the Urge Coupe acknowledges the special needs of elders. Passengers rise and hold onto the grab bar as the seat rotates clockwise to offer toilet (A), storage bin (B), toilet flush water tank (C), and waste tank (D) options. Seat cushions (B, C and D) are lifted to provide access to a bin. Each bin may be detached and removed using its bin handle. If the toilet is used during travel, a fan is activated, pushing fumes to the toilet exhaust vents on the roof.

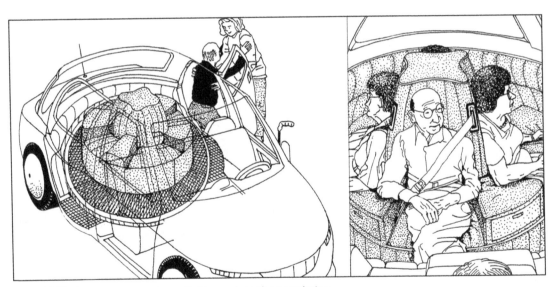

ROTASEAT   A greater percentage of old people in the population results in a demand for products like the automobile Rotaseat. A motor-driven circular seat for four that adapts to wide-body cars and vans, it gives stiff, infirm passengers easy access to the curb and minimizes joint strain when climbing out.

CUSTODAY CARE Stiff insurance regulations relating to the handling and release of children at child care centers lead to the adoption of safe transfer vehicles. The wheels are locked until an authorized parent or guardian inserts a card into a slot in the machine. Tampering with a child sets off an alarm.

It's a dangerous world out there

In the late 1990's and beyond, danger is everywhere. Fear is palpable. Crime is out of control. Threats of terrorism are on the increase. Locking the house doors, which fifty years earlier had been optional, has by now become not only a necessity, but often a hopelessly inadequate step taken to keep the "criminal element" at bay. The latest technologies are applied for the creation of unique and effective personal, home and public safety products and systems.

WHAT TO WATCH FOR:

❏ Personal ray detectors give off a warning sound when there is nearby nuclear radiation, radon gas, or excessive UV radiation.

❏ Glue guns stop criminals literally in their tracks.

❏ Porcupine-emulating or electric eel-emulating apparel repel attackers aggressively. One outfit emits a horrible smell.

❏ Children are each assigned their own combination desk and hiding chamber at school.

❏ The portion of the floor directly in front of the teller's cage in a bank is a trap door.

FAUX BODY SHAPE UNDERGARMENTS A special inner body-shaping garment can be worn in neighborhoods where harassment is common. Men may need to appear larger and more threatening. Women may want to seem old or unattractive, though they may then be subjected to purse-snatching.

STREET ESCAPE CLOSETS Human safes are installed in districts where street crime is common. Placed a block apart, they are impenetrable by thugs once the door is locked from the inside. Conduits for fresh air ducts as well as for electricity and phone lines are inaccessible from the outside.

SAFE SIDEWALK PASSAGE Entry ways to inner city apartments in inner cities are outfitted with wheeled, fenced connection tubes that interface with specially designed taxis.

PERSONAL REARVIEW MIRRORS A sense of omnipresent danger unsettles many who find it necessary to leave their homes, autos, or businesses for a walk on the sidewalk. Rearview mirrors become a standard personal accessory as part of eyeglasses (A), or tailored to fit inside a lapel (B).

SECURISLEEP Sleeping in a car at a freeway roadside rest, an occasional necessity for tired travelers, is less worrisome when one parks inside a lockable, rental auto "cage."

REMOTE PATROL The risk for highway police in stopping errant or suspicious drivers is eliminated when "long arm of the law" vehicles are in use. The extension arm places a camera, interactive video screen, and a summons printer against the window of the driver, who must insert a magnetically-coded card in a slot.

PUBLIC SHAMING VAN Public shaming, a practice in use in China, is adopted in the U.S. Accused criminals must sit inside a specially-designed police van behind clear, bullet-proof glass. They are handcuffed and paraded before the public. A placard shows their name and describes their crime.

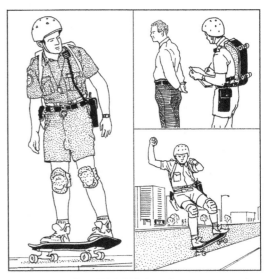

POLICE ON SKATEBOARDS A new generation of police persons brings a handy skill to their occupation: skateboarding. Patrols make spectacular sidewalk arrests and are applauded by onlookers for stylish maneuvers.

INTIMIDATING AUTO STYLES Auto stylists respond to an angry, defensive attitude in Americans by offering them cars with a road-hugging, angular, "tank" look in mottled, spattered, or camouflage colors. Cars have narrow slots for windows, body armor, bulletproof glass and teargas guns.

MUNICIPAL INCARCERIDE Municipalities purchase buses designed to thwart gang fights, harassment, foul language, and intimidation of passengers. Some buses place each passenger in separate locker, with a door that locks when wheels move; others have a jail (and jailer) at the back of the bus.

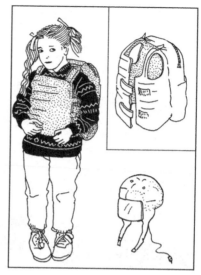

PEDESTRIAN OUTFITS Angry citizens appear on sidewalks in groups, wearing a queer melange of police shields and body armor. Fashion designers, sensing a trend, come out with wildly patterned styles in cheerful colors.

BACK-TO-SCHOOL ARMOR In the fall, back-to-school newspaper ads remind parents to replace scruffy or outgrown bookpack-vest armor and bullet-proof hats with new designs for the coming school year.

BUS ARMOR A bus ride can be frightening for all who anticipate a possible attack by a group of young strangers. Bus armor gives the wearer an improved sense of personal safety even if in the summer the armor makes one feel hot and sweaty.

PLEXIGARDS Getting mugged on a transit ride is no longer feared on systems where pull-down, impact-resistant Plexigards are standard car equipment. Riders can even doze off safely while commuting.

ENDANGERED PERSON ESCORT People who fear for their life request a Links escort. Armed guards guide an explosion-proofed cart from a Links truck into a building, protecting the body of a businessperson, politician, drug lord, or fearful citizen.

WALKING SHROUD It is a pleasant experience walking in the neighborhood when one is protected by a Walking Shroud. Effortless to steer, and relatively lightweight, the Shroud is impact- and bullet-resistant. It includes a built-in mobile phone employing the latest TDMA technology.

JOGGER SAFETY SHROUD Women joggers buy or rent bullet-resistant, floorless electric runabouts as security shrouds to use while jogging in public parks. They steer them with handle controls, and can adjust the speed to match their running pace. If in trouble, they simply sit down, draw up their feet, and drive away.

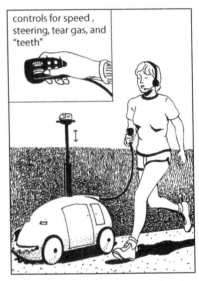

SIMUDOG Some women prefer the reliability and multiple-weapons capability of a Simudog when out running, over that of an actual dog. It can be maneuvered quickly to attack in any direction.

CAPTAIN'S RUN Home styles for the affluent continue a trend toward elaborate, complicated roofs. Some support a modem version of a captain's walk, widened and reinforced for jogging. Residents step out from an attic door to sunbathe, spy on neighbors, eat breakfast, or run laps.

HOME SOLICITOR INTERROGATION ROOM Solicitor interrogation rooms are a feature frequently requested by new home buyers. A bulletproof viewing window (or a one-way mirror) is paired with a sliding security tray, similar to systems used at banks and all-night gas stations.

PORCH CELL Porch cells prove a nasty surprise to intruders, solicitors, or Bible salespersons. Their revolving fake doors and doormats collapse automatically during an attempted break-in, or manually if a suspicious move is made. There is no way to get out of the cell until police arrive.

AIRLINE LUGGAGE PLANE The Luggage Plane Project is a national effort to prevent terrorists from sneaking plastic explosives aboard planes. Luggage-carrying, radar-guided flying wings are connected by a tether to passenger planes. Passengers must remove clothing and don pocket-less smocks.

MOTORCYCLE EXTENDER   A motorcycle with an extender occupies the same road space as a small automobile. The extender gives limited protection in minor collisions. The tubular structure provides spaces for an attache case, camping gear, or shopping bags, and serves as a "kickstand" for parking.

CAR EXTENDER   Driver training classes teach desirable car lengths between cars for safe driving at varied speeds. But cautious drivers find it easier to purchase autos with the car extender feature. Pneumatic pistons add six feet to the car's length.

INFLATABLE CRASH SUIT SYSTEM In 1988, air bags were first offered as standard equipment on US automobiles. Some drivers and passengers did not trust them, fearing the maiming effect of an explosive bag thrust in their face, or worse, a bag failing to open at the moment of impact. Buyers of the newly-introduced Chrashler Air Protection System vehicle view themselves as early adopters of a system that offers a warranty (limited) of crash survival. The car comes standard with a massive, whole-body bumper. Suits are inflated by a built-in air pump system. When all suits are fully inflated and helmets are donned, it is safe to proceed ahead.

Planning communities for threats and danger

It's difficult to relax in America anymore. There is simply too much to worry about. You take your life in your hands, as it were, just walking down an urban sidewalk. Taking a nap in the park, or letting your child play on the swings while you sleep, is no more than a cultural memory of an earlier, safer time.

It was inevitable, therefore, that a variety of sidewalk machines would be available to those who could afford to purchase them. These should be called Sidedrive, not Sidewalk, machines!

And you think twice before you take your child to the local park. It is often safer to let your child play in the Drive Up Playground. Moreover, increasingly park and recreation planners must design plans that meet the needs of the police, whose ideal park is an empty, flat, grassed space with nothing for a criminal to hide behind.

ARMORED STREET AND SIDEWALK MACHINES   No sidewalk is safe in the new America. Old rules forbidding the use of bicycles and similar small vehicles on sidewalks are scrapped and Sidewalk Machines are not only permitted but increasingly seen threading slowly through a sidewalk crowd. Similarly, no one is surprised to share the road with a Street Machine driven by an ordinary citizen that features gun mounts and maximum-thickness explosion protection.

DRIVE UP PLAYGROUND Lacking access to safe open space or play yards, poor families let their children climb aboard a Drive Up Playground. A pleasant sound, like that of the Good Humor ice cream truck, announces the approach of the mobile playground, which parks for an hour.

WALLED MINIPARKS Walled, guarded miniparks offer a safe place for children to play. Family members or relatives must register to accompany a child. The registration information is checked with national police registries before an admission card is issued. Parents, as well as security guards, observe children at play.

Before

After

PARKS DESIGNED BY POLICE DEPARTMENTS Dismal, featureless police-friendly parks are designed according to Public Safety Standards for Landscaping Placement and Trimming. Decried by horticulturalists, landscape planners and civil libertarians, the parks disallow aesthetic mounding, hedges, glens, and low-growing trees which might offer hiding places for criminals and perverts. Paths are aligned to maximize lines-of-sight for firing a gun.

FACADE BUNKS Owners of major public buildings are required by the Homeless Law to commission architects to modify their building facades so as to include spaces for overnight beds for the homeless.

Safe places to hide out and sleep

There is an unresolved disparity between the life opportunities of people on the fast track to career advancement and information access, and of unemployed or low-paid menial workers who serve them. As crime and violence worry many, the clearest indicator of social status becomes simply where one sleeps.

WHAT TO WATCH FOR:

- ❑ Guards-for-hire stand by your bed as you sleep.

- ❑ Sleep hoods are sold that "put you to sleep" within minutes by inducing sleep brain-wave patterns.

- ❑ Beds are made that facilitate "conscious dreams," out-of-body travel, and psychic trips. A WakeTape brings you back slowly and safely.

- ❑ "Burrowers" are a class of forgotten, homeless persons who live in holes dug in the woods and fields, and who beg for food along scenic highways.

- ❑ Drunks, derelicts and the homeless who sleep in the open use "alarm-bags." Breaking into a bag sets off a piercing alarm.

HOMELESS LOTS Used car sales lots, no longer viable because pre-1995 cars are illegal on public streets, are subdivided to form open stalls for homeless campers. Rules: no fires or camp stoves in stalls, no shooting of guns, no alcoholic beverages or drugs, and no music or loud conversation after 10 PM.

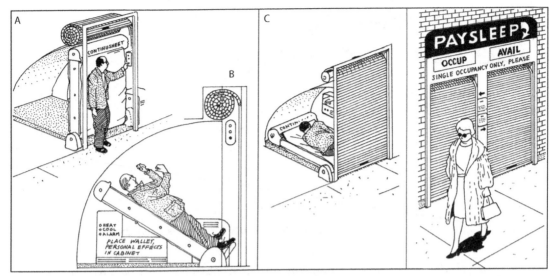

SLEEPING IN THE WALLS When very tired, drunk, dazed or drugged individuals feel the urgent need to "fall" into bed while downtown, they search for an empty Paysleep and hope for enough mental clarity to correctly insert dollar bills into a wall slot. A fresh sheet, rolled up inside a wide dispenser, is made for each customer. The procedure is simple. Insert four five dollar bills to raise the rolling security gate (A), press the first button to initiate the sheet-changing roll mechanism, and then the second button to slowly lower the bed to the horizontal (B). Once inside (C), fall asleep.

PUBLIC SLEEPING CONCESSIONS The number of "permanently poor" Americans grows. It comprises people who lack desirable skills in a shrinking, selective economy. Notions persist of the poor as lazy victims of their own bad habits. Lazy Susans, or Lazy Sams are the names given by the public to sleeping concessions installed by businesses in rundown downtown buildings. These offer more privacy than rule-bound hostels and shelters, and better protection than parks or sidewalks.

PERSON MINI-STORAGE It is not much fun to be an American when you spend each night at a Person Mini-storage. There is only enough space for one or two people with their shopping carts. A public rest room and launderette is provided for each floor.

PLANNED HOBO APARTMENT UNITS Bridges and dams are retrofitted with quarters for vagrants. Government-licensed hobos receive rent-free living space in exchange for daily duties manning terrorist-watch lookouts.

UNDERGROUND HOSTELS Park and recreation departments merge with social welfare departments once public parks are designated as the logical place for housing the homeless. Underground dormitories, Catahomes, are built beneath parks, and auto parking structures are redesigned as rent-free apartments without walls.

INFORMATION SPECIALTY BUMS When large numbers of computer-literate persons cannot find employment, a class of itinerant information specialists forms. It moves, gypsy-like, from place to place in cities with warmer climates. Portable office services are rendered by street vendors who work door-to-door or set up their "office" in "computer user" parks. Vigilante justice is quickly meted out for the group's most serious crime–computer equipment theft. Parks offer rental lockers for storing lap tops and printers. Hand trucks, pushcarts, minivans, and motorcycles become information services shops.

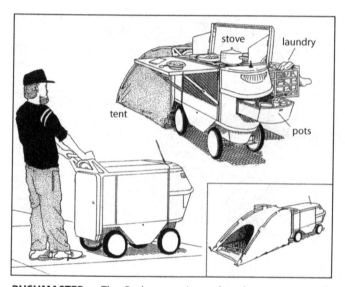

PUSHMASTER The Pushmaster is marketed to economically disadvantaged persons, loners, cranks, and hermits. It is sold, rented, or given out free under local government programs for the homeless. It is so much more useful than a shopping cart that fights break out over it, and it is often stolen. Pushmasters can be safely left inside locked rental cages.

DESK TENT Electronically-literate graduates of Army "learn a trade" programs, or of community college computer courses, wander as itinerant, skilled bums with no place to sleep, carrying live-in workstations.

STARVING KNOWLEDGE WORKERS Well-educated, over-educated Americans slip to the bottom of the nation's economy as the gap between rich and poor grows. It is not uncommon to see offers of manuscript typing in exchange for food. The worker is usually paid in food first, and then given the work task.

PORTABLE PULLMAN   A disheartening sight in American towns around the turn of the century is of dispirited, homeless persons dragging their architect-designed portable homes along sidewalks and gutters. Their Portable Pullmans look like oversized mailboxes and are pulled like a child's wagon.

PULLMAN PARK   Public and for-profit mobile homeless parks are built in the outskirts of cities. Families and individuals commingle with camaraderie, despite hopeless personal situations, in a scene that looks like a reunion camp-out of a tired, unfortunate family. Co-op homeless parks have strict rules and usually self-police for illegal weapons, drugs and communicable diseases, yet offer nightly campfires with entertainment, free movies, and "citizen education." Political and religious haranguing often stirs them to form themselves into political coalitions, or to ponder the sinful causes of their plight.

MOTORLESS HOME Successful homeless persons, as their first step back up the ladder to "homefulness," purchase plush, fully equipped, motorless homes. Also, hermits and religious renunciates buy them.

PERSON-PROPELLED VAN Stair-climbing exercise machines are adapted for propelling ultralight microvans. Geared low, the vans creep along city bike lanes at 2 mph and park in policed lots at night. An auxiliary motor is available for situations requiring a burst of speed, for hill climbing, or when the operator feels tired.

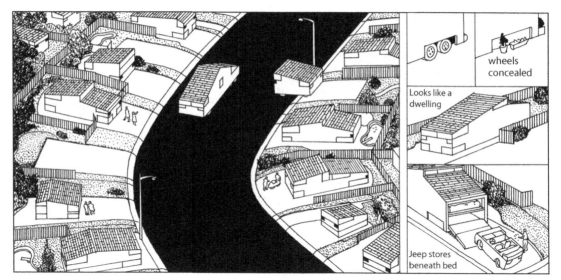

Labels in image: wheels concealed · Looks like a dwelling · Jeep stores beneath bed

THE MOTORHOME SUBURB   The motorhome is justly criticized by frugal citizens and environmentalists for its poor gas mileage and bloated image of excess. Yet when new neighborhoods are laid out in which the motorhome is also the home, the accusation of waste and duplication of resources is undercut. The homes are sold at a subdivision sales lot, and are designed to match a set of Codes, Covenants and Restrictions (CC&Rs). With concealed wheels (Rule 13A), the homes do not look mobile. One model even includes a rear bedroom in which a Jeep-like vehicle, with a fold-flat windshield, is parked inside, beneath a large bed.

MOTORROOMS   People who have little to do except travel may invest in homes with matching, fitted motor homes. These "motorrooms" park snugly against the main house when not on the road, where they serve as self-contained apartments. They are driven out as the season and investment income dictate.

STORE 'N' STAY Public storage motels link personal furniture storage to temporary living in unfurnished rooms. Belongings are kept within revolving, compartmentalized storage rooms, accessible at any hour for inspired furniture rearrangement projects.

Separate hoses are attached for electricity, phone and modem, TV, water and drain.

ADD-A-ROOM   Unpredictable incomes lead homeowners to attach Add-A-Room connectors to their homes. These self-contained studio apartments can be hooked up to house utilities, leveled and readied for occupancy in less than an hour. They are suitable for renters or for visiting relatives. The connector hose attaches easily. It includes hoses and wires for electricity, phone, modem, TV, and water, and drains for toilet and sink.

SWIMMING MOAT   Though swimming pool construction is curtailed in drought- prone regions, contractors continue to install pools for wealthy clients. Swimming moats are built at the time of the home's construction. They have drawbridges for entryways and garages with doorbridges–a variation on the drawbridge–that are controlled with garage openers. Unauthorized entry is effectively discouraged, since burglars do not wish to contemplate climbing slippery walls in wet running shoes, or wading in 5-foot-deep water while balancing delicate electronic appliances overhead. Posted signs suggest the added possibility of serious electric shock.

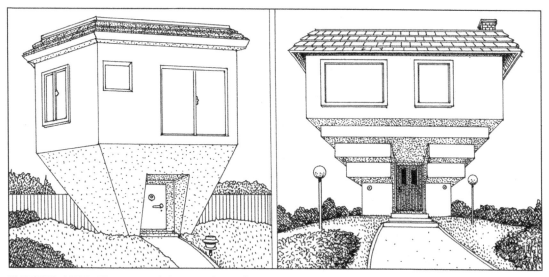

THE PEER-AMID   The pyramid shape is classically narrow at the top and wide at the bottom. The Peer-amid Home, on the other hand, offers the opposite design, with a narrowed, windowless base that is perfect for watching the approach of possible criminals from the safety of the upper story. The home sits "amid" other, conventionally-styled homes and by design seems uninviting as compared with neighbors' homes. Some residents complain, however, that the design is flawed, since persons with ill intent can hide out of sight beneath the large overhang.

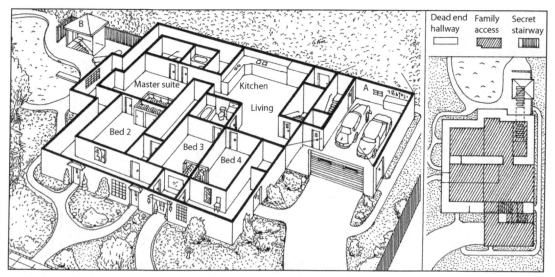

HOME-INVASION-THWARTING LABYRINTH FLOOR PLAN The wealthy are never perfectly safe from home invasion and break-and-enter crimes unless they purchase a home with a labyrinth floor plan. The plan thoroughly confuses burglars and home invasion gangs. It's numerous doors lead to dead end hallways and empty rooms. Residents gain entry via secret stairways hidden inside a garage storage closet (A), and a swimming pool shower and change room (B).

UNDERGROUND BEDROOM A sense that one may not be safe inside one's dwelling motivates homeowners to install backyard underground bedrooms, approached through secret passageways. Stocked with food, television, phone and a portable camping toilet, they promise a sound sleep.

HOME PERIMETER DOG RUN A novel way of improving home security is one that makes use of a dog's natural alertness and sensitivity. A dog runway/balcony that includes a dog house, tightly surrounds a home. Touching the metal structure anywhere causes a vibration that a sleeping dog can detect.

FEAR FURNITURE At the always popular Fear Furniture showroom, many new models of hiding furniture are displayed. Each year, prospective buyers inspect the latest models. Completed models of the Fear Home are also shown. They feature false panels, secret upstairs rooms, escape hatches, and hidden corridors. A typical example of a new piece of fear furniture is one that is bullet-proofed and sound-proofed–lest a hiding resident's breathing gives away their location–and contains a hidden telephone with the "muffle-speak" feature that allows one to speak to a 911 operator undetected.

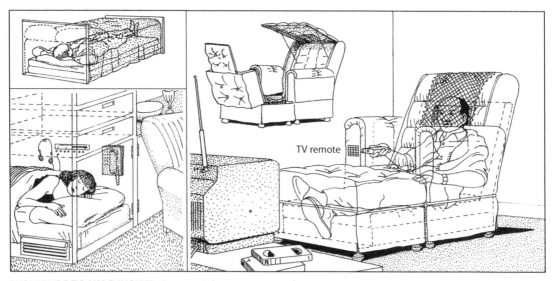

FURNITURE TO HIDE INSIDE Furniture designers create furniture a person can climb inside at night. Fearing forced home entry, people are willing to sit as if invisible inside oversized recliners to watch favorite television programs. Beds are built hidden beneath larger, apparently empty beds or inside walls as pullout bed drawers.

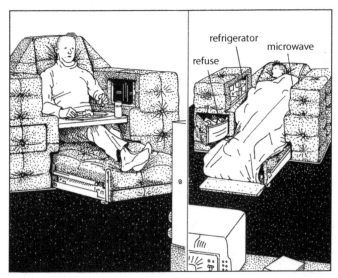

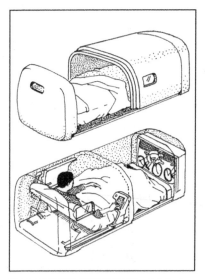

TELEVISION LIFE-SUPPORT SYSTEM Cautious Americans, sensing danger at every turn, may seek the passive, indrawn personal life of the television spectator, or "couch potato." Superchairs are sold that can be customized to meet almost every need.

TV SLEEPING CHAMBERS Addiction to television, a disease, can lead individuals to buy bullet proofed, sound-deadening television-watching cocoons.

HOME BULLET PROOFING Nightly gunshot sounds ruin the peacefulness of suburban neighborhoods, and residents sleep with earplugs and pile metal furniture between their bed and street side walls. Home bullet proofing services guarantee their special window glass and in-the-wall padding.

POTATO COUCH ROOM GROUP Unique, and at times humorous, furniture groupings are sold, often with the cocooning-at-home theme. The Potato Couch Room Group, a visual pun that employs realistic-looking yet comfortable potato shapes, is popular. The Spud Comforter zips up for warmth.

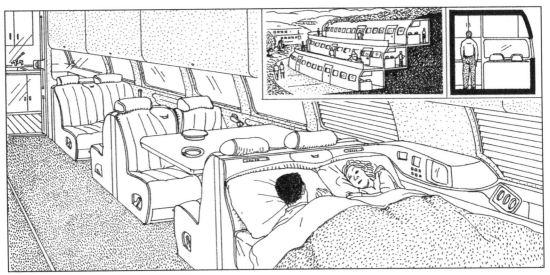

AUTOMOBILE-STYLE DWELLINGS A zany fad of living in semi-underground, automobile-style homes moves critics to wonder if the nation has lost its collective mind. The narrow homes are sunny corridors decorated in vinyl, Naugahyde and painted metal, where residents play audiotapes of running engines or watch videos of traffic jams.

STUDIO HOMES Local governments are petitioned to assign unused public properties as space for dwellings for the homeless. Studio homes, built by manufacturers of motor homes and job-site toilets, are dropped on land subdivided into micro-plots.

AGRICULTURAL WORKER HOMES Architects are enlisted by government agricultural commissions to design livable sleeping areas for migrant workers to replace their tar papered- and cardboard-covered underground burrows. One design shows communal bedrooms mounted on pillars above the crops.

HOMES PURCHASED BY THE ROOM Young people who have been locked out of the home-purchasing tradition may now put a down payment on a home that they purchase one room at a time.

BOLT-ON HOMES CUL-DE-SAC The new economy has the effect of exaggerating one's angst over reduced financial circumstances, even while allowing one to be more open about one's status. In a Bolt-On Homes subdivision, residents are tolerant of new homeowners who can only afford the Starter unit.

ROOMS ADDED A PIECE AT A TIME The starter unit of a home purchased by the room is a studio bedroom with bathroom and "hot plate mini-kitchen." Bolt-On Homes, for example, first locates the starter unit on a large construction pad with connectors, fittings and pipes in place for rooms that will be added later, as income improves.

MENACING ROOFS Prosperous adults who as teenagers sported nose rings, orange hair and offensive haircuts "keep up with the Joneses" by building homes with aesthetically upsetting and menacing roofs that are costly to construct and repair. These punk roofs have no noteworthy insulating or protective properties.

Single family home

MEGA-McMANSIONS Warrens of multi-roomed, palace-like single family homes are built which extend for blocks without separating yards. Second-story walkways connect mansion wings for parties and intimate relations. These homes offer neither pleasant grounds nor privacy but give the wealthy a sense of sharing and togetherness.

CONSTRUCTED BY WHIM Tracts of fantasy homes are built that make use of the maximum plastic potential of construction materials. Buyers, expressing their emotions in a builder's "play with clay" room, are guided by designer-psychologists to design their home with halls to crawl through, bedrooms to slide out of, or front doors to fall in.

Do you wish to discuss your attitude towards your mother? Do you have tunnel collapse nightmares? Any phobias I need to know about?

DESIGNER-PSYCHOLOGIST Plans for a Whim Home originate in the clay studio, under the guidance of a designer-psychologist. The client may discuss personal preferences and issues, while working with clay.

SINGLE-FAMILY TOWERS As land prices escalate in desirable living areas, builders of single-family homes for the upper middle class begin to build skyward on tiny lots. Four- and five-story towers are outfitted with elevators, dumbwaiters and video systems. Yards offer no privacy, as neighbors can look down into them.

DOUBLE-WALLED COMMUNITIES   In an action that sends America several giant steps backwards to the Middle Ages, land developers gain approval from planning departments to build double-walled communities for wealthy executives. Tenant-entrepreneur employment offices near outer guard stations examine applicants wishing to live and provide exclusive services in shops inside the walls. No service–housecleaning, plumbing, or baby-sitting–is done by anyone who is not an indentured, live-in trades person.

MAXIMUM SECURITY RETIREMENT   The most futuristic-looking neighborhoods in America are the maximum-security retirement communities. They feature smooth walls that cannot be climbed, robots that walk dogs, bulletproof glass-enclosed jogging and horse riding tracks, and armed shuttle vans.

MONITOWERS   Neighborhood Monitowers, with video cameras scanning streets and yards below, are constructed to supplement helicopter surveillance. The towers are staffed by security guards who watch monitors, as exercise classes and child care programs are conducted in ground-level rooms below.

FEAR COMPLEX The Fear Complex, a Home In Detention Environment (HIDE), allows law-abiding citizens, who are not insane, to be temporarily or permanently placed in the compound for their own security and safety. These compounds look and function much like maximum security prisons, except that inmates enter by choice, and the "criminal element" is locked outside rather than inside the gates. Inmates are free to leave at any time. The atmosphere is quiet, cooperative, friendly and non-aggressive, and free from doctrinal harangues and psychiatric probing. Principal activity areas are libraries, craft centers and garden plots.

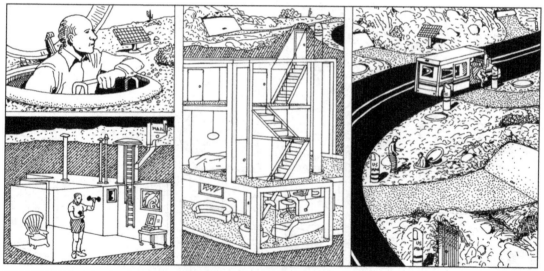

SUBTERRANEAN DWELLINGS FOR DROPOUTS Pestering, surveillance, and a bad economy become too much for some individuals, who not only opt out of society, but choose a home with the least above-ground visibility. In the DropOut Homes subdivision, all that is visible above ground is a mailbox, a manhole-like entrance lid, and a garage door. Living below ground, a resident is not visible to spy planes except on days when he or she emerges to fetch a package that's too large to drop down the mail chute. By special statute in some states, residents do not need to record their name on the deed. In some places, everyone is named John or Jane Doe!

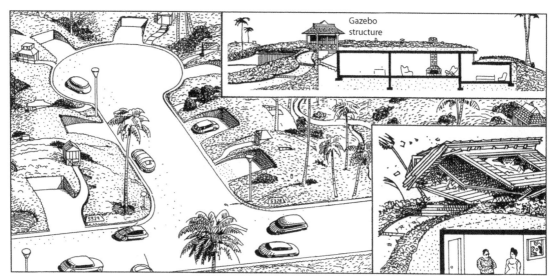

HURRICANE-PROOF HOMES The first significant tracts of underground homes are developed in Louisiana and other Gulf states, where hurricanes often wreak havoc. Entrance to these houses is through a conspicuous and stylish gazebo structure that is inexpensively replaced if knocked over in a storm.

DOME HOME COMMUNITY Dome-shaped homes like those made by Dome Home Builders, are resistant to fire, earthquake, cyclone, and hurricanes. They are extremely energy efficient. New neighborhoods, flattened one too many times by a tornado, are rebuilt as a pleasant subdivision of dome homes. While the home shape seems comical and cartoonish, no one is laughing at the designs after dome homes are the only dwellings that survive a major tornado. For safety, residents learn they must stay clear of window openings, which can be breached by a telephone pole or pieces of the roof of a nearby supermarket, flying through the air at 150 mph.

WEATHER-RESPONSIVE BUILDINGS Homes are constructed that can withstand the worst possible cyclone or hurricane. As weather worsens, the second-story roofs and clerestory windows are seen to slowly sink on pneumatic pillars into the first floor for protection.

GREENHOUSE-EFFECT HOMES Tales of impending rising ocean levels lead coastal area home buyers to purchase Greenhouse-Effect Homes. They are four-story towers with a lifeboat in a third-story barn, from which they can safely contemplate rising waters.

SUPERROOFS The increase in cases of home destruction by falling satellite and airplane parts leads fearful homeowners to have Superroofs constructed. These are reinforced steel structures topped with layered, four-feet-thick shock-absorbing pads.

HARD TENTS A softer generation of car campers rejects lightweight backpacker's tents in favor of impact-resistant, "party time" hard tents. Windblown tree limbs or inebriated fellow campers cannot cause harm if they fall on a sleeping camper. For transport the tents fold or nest to fit inside or on top of a car.

Homes for new lifestyles

The typical new home in a subdivision begins to change. New homes are designed that acknowledge the radical transformations taking place in family affinities and groupings: There are lesbian parents, divorced couples, transgender couples and "friends with benefits." Old ideas of head-of-household and husband-and-wife are no longer relevant in home design.

DIVORCE-PLEX HOMES Some newlyweds frankly acknowledge the statistical likelihood that they will become divorced eventually, and purchase homes with mirror-image spaces that can be divided into separate living units by lowering a built-in sound-proofed central wall. If tensions escalate, the couple can decide to live separately on a trial basis, or permanently.

HOMES FOR DAY/NIGHT WORKERS Changing work patterns affect all aspects of life, including home design. An increasingly common practice of home sharing by unrelated persons who work different shifts leads to homes designed for the needs of both day and night workers. Night workers occupy the shaded, sound-proofed rear quarters with few windows, while day workers sleep in the other half. Both day and night workers have access to a common kitchen and living/entertainment room.

CLOSED SYSTEM NEIGHBORHOODS In "closed system" neighborhoods recycling consciousness reaches a fervor. Neighborhood entry stations are set up to check for thefts of home siding and precious metals, and to inventory materials to assess the "potential for neighborhood good" in each piece of scrap hauled away.

The green community

As conscientious folks continue to try to "save the Earth" by buying bleach-free toilet paper, some individuals and groups get increasingly anxious and serious about living in harmony with nature.

WHAT TO WATCH FOR:

- ❏ One night in jail is the automatic fine for carelessly tossing out an aluminum can.
- ❏ Employees at many firms are requested to donate break times to tilling the company vegetable gardens.
- ❏ Nightly television programs show offenders who "confess" to wasting fossil fuel while taking casual, weekend pleasure trips, or when running unnecessary errands.
- ❏ Home exercise equipment is sold with "juicer" and "grains-grinding" attachments.
- ❏ Going to church on Sundays is replaced by a new national habit of "getting quiet and feeling one's connection with the Earth and stars."
- ❏ There are shower and personal washing systems that use no water.
- ❏ Subdivisions are laid out by geomancer-planners, who position home plots in harmony with earth, magnetic, water-flow, and etheric forces.

NEW AGE MODEL HOMES The Green ethic creeps into all facets of home layout and landscaping design. New home buyers demand root cellars, compost bins, solar water distillers, built-in solar cookers, front yard vegetable patches and non-off-gassing building construction and decorating materials.

HOME SERVICE BINS In some new suburban neighborhoods, compartmentalized bins combine in one place the usual collection of boxes, bins and heaps available for items delivered to, or hauled away from, the home.

NEIGHBORHOOD SHARING As waves of scarcity roll through neighborhoods, sharing stands appear. Families may own homes yet lack food or water; have a tree with too many apricots but no shoes for their children.

SUBURBS FOR THE OVERLY SENSITIVE New disciplines emerge, replacing outmoded city and land planning occupations. There are now Siddhi Planners and Chakra-tuning home siting experts. Subdivisions advertise standing stones. Room layout and home siting is in accord with Feng Shui and geomancy principles. Homes are sited to avoid negative radiations along geopathic stress zones.

SOLAR COOK-A-MAT Community solar cooking stations look like laundromats. Rules are posted for cleanliness and users are urged to lock the glass lids with keys provided at an office. Potluck parties feature solar-cooked food, solar-distilled water, and Sun Tea.

DUMPSTER DINING The Tossed Salad Cafe is a darkly amusing name given to these specially-designed dumpsters that offer a fold-down table and bench. For food, diners must "dumpster dive." The choicest locations for one of these Tossed Salad Cafes is behind or near a supermarket or restaurant.

TRASH FOR SALE   An enlightened public re-examines concepts of "trash" and "waste." There is rising global awareness of the limited space for dumpsites, and of finite world resources. Products are recycled for their raw materials or are reused. Dump sites are mined for elegant, rare finds.

DOWNSCALE SHOPPING CENTERS   Sales of used items climb as purchases of expensive new products decline. Derelict shopping centers are reopened, specializing in second-hand things.

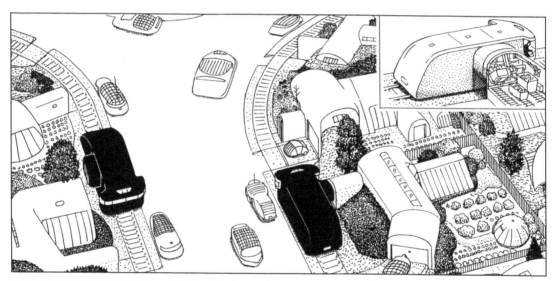

AUTOMATED UTILITIES   Unusual in both design and appearance are communities with automated (no driver) Utility Toilers that integrate mail and package delivery, garbage, trash, recyclables and clippings collection. Running day and night, they move quietly on tracks, halting at homes to make deliveries and take on trash or mail.

ALUMINUM CAN HARVESTING KIT Unemployed or environmentally conscious people scan gutters and ditches for aluminum cans while riding on mountain bikes equipped with lockable bins. Within reach behind the seat is a long-handled tool for grabbing cans. Bin lids are opened with handlebar levers.

RECYCLE POLICE　　Failing to sort your garbage, using too much gasoline, or secretly operating a freon-based air conditioner become serious crimes. Having a career as a Recycle Policeman is as honorable as being a professional basketball player.

BOXED NEWSPAPER CONSTRUCTION　Building codes in some cities are modified to permit erection of homes with 16-inch walls, insulated with stacked, 14-inch-wide boxes of newspapers sprayed with fire retardant. Newspaper publishers give away the boxes free, and run ads showing homeowners who "built their home with the News."

HOME COMES APART Upscale families build homes that periodically appear to come apart, as giant bins, filled with such items as aluminum cans left over from 100-guest parties, or clippings from ten acres of landscape pruning, drive themselves to the street.

SOLAR-CHARGED ELECTRIC MOWER Lawn seed hybrids are created that yield slow-growing grasses that need less frequent mowing. When it's necessary to trim the grass, a solar-charged cordless electric mower is taken out of its charging shed.

JUNK MAIL INSULATION Before junk mail is banned because its use depletes world forests and nonrenewable fossil fuel reserves, a new "useful" junk mail is printed with nontoxic inks on fire-retardant, recycled paper and offered as sound-deadening and insulating material for home interior walls.

FOOT-PEDALED HOT WALL CLOTHES DRYER Some Natural Systems Homes offer a foot-pedaled, drum dryer built into a south-facing wall. The dryer is warmed by a solar-heated, rectangular water-filled box. An insulated panel drops in the evening, or when outside temperatures cool.

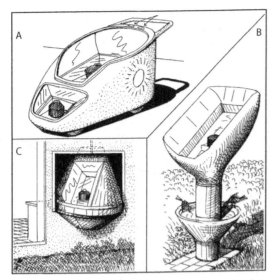

DESIGNER SUN OVENS   Designers of solar cooker ovens dump the boxed, science-project aesthetic to create outdoor solar appliances that beautify the backyard. There's the solar cooker on wheels (A), the self-orienting garden oven with birdbath (B), and the sun-tracking Lazy Solar Susan in-the-wall oven (C).

SKYLIGHT OVEN   New kitchens incorporate both high- and low-tech appliances. A low-tech solar oven is part of a skylight in a south-facing roof or wall. An insulated black metal oven insert, holding a large black pot of carrots and potatoes, is raised up into the skylight for worry-free cooking.

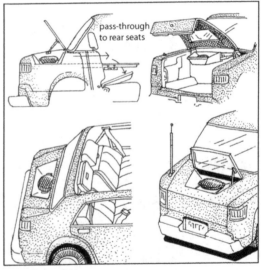

CAR-B-Q   In summer, owners of Solar Cooking Coupes drive home in the evening with a hot meal in the rooftop oven. While they worked indoors in an air-conditioned building, their car's solar oven caught the sun's rays, trapped heat beneath a transparent lid, and cooked a potato and carrot stew.

SOLAR COOKER TRUNK   Cooking smells exit the trunk via the tiny solar cooker exhaust pipe. A wired temperature sensor and alarm connect to a dashboard read-out, showing elapsed cooking time and current (and maximum) pot temperature. The pot is locked in place to prevent spills while driving.

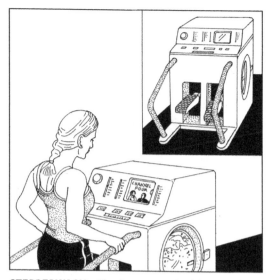

WASH CYCLE A line of Retro-Active machines that use no electricity offers users the chance to practice energy independence while they exercise. The Wash Cycle features pedal-operated washing and a hand wringer, and connects to a passive solar water heater and outdoor clothesline.

STEPPERWASH The Stepperwash claims to churn and cycle clothes adequately, when powered by a fit human. Settings for hot and cold, extended wash and drain functions are controlled by the exerciser. A TV set is included in the control panel to ward off boredom.

PEDAL-WASH Similar in design to the Retro-Active washing machine, the Pedal-Wash can be used at any hour of the day, and even when the electric power is down. This gives the user the sense of having accomplished a task in a virtuous manner, with the side benefit of staying in shape.

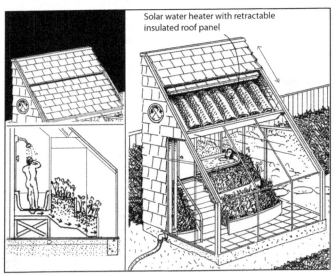

DROUGHT-WISE HOMES Sporadic drought conditions spawn unique home design features. Home buyers in drought-prone regions prefer homes with rain gutters integrated with rain runoff tanks and drip-irrigation lines.

BATHING GREENHOUSE The Bathing Greenhouse was designed to meet multiple purposes. Water for bath and shower is heated by solar drums built into the roof that are insulated by a retractable roof panel during cool or cloudy weather. Waste water from the bathtub and shower drains into a drip irrigation system that waters greenhouse plants.

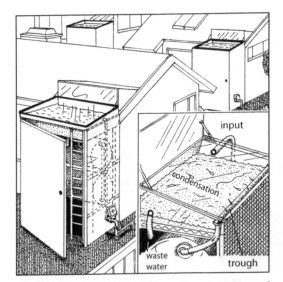

SOLAR WATER DISTILLERS Horror stories of pathogens, pesticides and toxic metals in tap water lead homeowners to attach solar water "distillation factories" to their homes. Sun-distilled water drips into sterile tanks. A timer floods the units with fresh water daily, flushing out old water for use on plants.

USED-WATER HOLDING TANK Used-water holding tanks are built inside walls and crawl spaces of new homes. Homes with "reuse" bathrooms and kitchens have instructions for when and what to flush, whether or not to save, how to monitor stored, used water, and how often to send water to the garden.

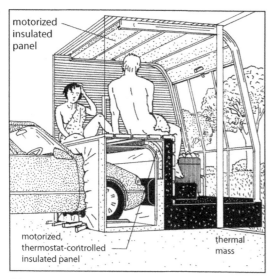

motorized
insulated
panel

motorized,
thermostat-controlled
insulated panel

thermal
mass

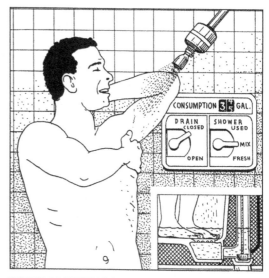

CONSUMPTION 3⅘ GAL.

DRAIN CLOSED / OPEN

SHOWER USED / MIX / FRESH

SOLAR/AUTO PREHEATED SAUNA After a day's work, owners of this sauna system drive their car into the garage, poke its engine compartment inside a heat-capturing cabinet, and jump into a sauna pre-warmed by athe sun. With the two supplemental heat sources, sauna heating costs are minimal.

WATER-RECYCLING SHOWER A shower that reuses its water is common in newer homes. You start and finish with fresh water, but mid-shower a control valve may be turned that allows for siphoning of the water collecting at your feet.

ONE WAY

Prior to reclamation

SUBURBAN RECLAMATION Neighborhood council meetings erupt into loud arguments, as "take back the soil" activists demand that suburban streets be torn up for use as communal vegetable gardens. City engineers are pressed into making plans that call for removal of street pavement, importation of topsoil, and dedication of easements across lawn-planted front yards for narrow, one-way "auto paths" made of semi-permeable paving materials.

In the labeled diagram:
rain collector and solar still
algae cultures
aquaculture
chicken pens
kitchen runs on methane

SURVIVOR HOMES Survivor Homes are the subject of envy and curiosity, and are shown in television documentaries as evidence of how serious things are getting. Distinctive because of their dark green rooftop algae ponds and fish-growing tanks, the homes are built low into the landscape, bunker-style. The subject of many jokes, the homes nonetheless have the theoretical capacity to support a family in a famine or food shortage. Chicken and egg production occupies a part of the living space, providing heat and methane to run kitchen appliances. It is a delicate living system, needing attentive maintenance.

FIRED CLAY HOMES Extremist communities are built that advocate rejection of many aspects of 20th-century technology. These differ from 1960's-style communes in attracting hard-working, well-organized citizens who are neither "laid back" nor relaxed, but are anxious to build a viable alternative society. An example is the cluster of communities in the American southwest with homes built of fired adobe, where purists park cars outside the city and walk or ride a bicycle to their home. Electric lighting, radio or television playing, or electrically-powered machines are forbidden in the community.

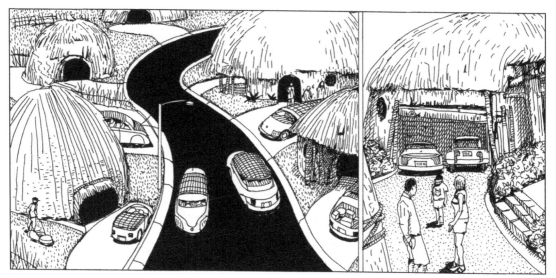

NATURAL, BIODEGRADABLE ARCHITECTURE   Travel to foreign countries creates a taste for features seen in native buildings but missing from style choices available to Americans. "Biodegradable" homes are built, featuring carefully crafted thatched roofs, beams made of tree trunks, and mud walls. Glue and nails are replaced by hemp rope, floors may be tamped earth.

MARRY A TREE FOR LIFE   Marriage to humans of another sex (or the same sex) proves so unsatisfactory and short-lived that sincere persons choose to marry a tree for life. The vows are spoken in a hushed, wooded setting, as one promises to risk one's life, if necessary, to save the life of one's tree spouse.

GREENIES   Joining the Greenies, young girls learn meditation, pledge allegiance to Mother Earth, and practice sorting trash. They receive credit for studying off-gassing, toxicity, pesticide tolerance, and heavy metal chromosome damage. On campouts, they apologize to Mother Earth before sitting on Her.

SOLAR-ELECTRIC INTRACONTINENTAL HIGHWAY   Early in the 21st century, Route 1SE is opened as the first leg in a vast intracontinental highway system designed for solar, electric, and other qualifying benign vehicles. Lanes are narrow, paving is smooth enough for bicycle tires, and Chargestops are located where solar cooking and solar battery recharging is best. Passively heated underground warming huts, free hostels (policed so they don't become "robbers roosts") are provided, as are free solar-distilled water and emergency solar-powered phones. Advertising billboards are outlawed except in locations directly above underground shops.

MINI-FREEWAY FOR MODEST VEHICLES   Mixing solar, battery-powered, and "alternative" light vehicles with heavy trucks and cars on public streets is unsafe. Once mini-freeways are erected, commuters leave their gasoline-engine cars at home and take 450-lb. solar-electric cars that they purchased or assembled at Solars for Singles clubs. In spite of 25 mph speed limits, a commute trip to a downtown job is faster than by gridlocked freeway. Usually the loudest sounds heard on these mini-freeways are the whir of tires or the mild whine of an electric motor. One may also hear a jingle, as commuters in solar-electrics signal bicyclists of their wish to pass.

PEDALTRAIN Transit Lite is a bold public program for construction of a system of 5-foot high, electric, pedal-assisted trains throughout suburban America. Reclining in cars light enough to be lifted by passengers back to the tracks in case of derailment, riders get a workout earning "energy-credits" that reduce, or even void their fare. Permission to board requires a pass, issued upon evidence of fitness from a doctor and a fitness-assessment specialist. Depots offer showers, change rooms, and an organic fruit and vegetable juices bar.

STANDING PEDALTRAIN The Standing PedalTrain makes up for two deficiencies of the sitting PedalTrain: it provides an aisle for walking around and stretching (in case of a leg cramp), and a rest room. The entire roof surface is covered with solar tiles which charge batteries during the day. The train runs on a hybrid-electric system, with power supplemented by both the pedaling efforts of passengers and the solar roof. The use of ultra-light materials in the construction of the modest passenger compartments makes this train more economical to operate than a normal passenger train. Critics complain that the train smells like a gym locker room!

SOLAR-POWERED AMERICA The United States begins to shift away from the direct use of fossil fuels and where possible, in favor of wind, hydro, and solar power. High-efficiency solar panels cover available surfaces, changing the appearance of American cities. Hydrogen fuel cell cars share the road with all-electric and hybrid gas-electric vehicles.

COMMUTERS ROWING CLUB Fragile commuter-powered cars are licensed for use on designated urban streets. Health clubs form around communal ownership of pedalcars and rowcars.

SOLAR HEATER ON A TRACK During daytime, 2-ton, water-filled solar heaters can be seen driving themselves to sunny corners of front or rear yards, only to retreat indoors at dusk to heat homes on cold nights. The heaters are encased in sturdy, heat-trapping plastic boxes.

INTRACONTINENTAL NON-HUMAN TRAIL To preserve continuity and integrity in animal migration routes, animal overpasses are constructed. They form an uninterrupted route across the U.S. Hikers may not use these trails; homeless persons are forbidden from camping out or hiding in the undergrowth.

FUELS PARADISE   As the nation struggles to buffer itself against the vagaries and international strife associated with dependence on fossil fuels, service stations offer a wider choice of fuels.   Autos are manufactured which can be powered by wood chips, coal, French fry grease, algae, and other exotic fuels.

INSTANT BATTERY EXCHANGE   Electric cars are criticized for their short range, which can leave a driver stranded. In very cold weather, batteries become markedly less efficient. New electric car models use a modular, industry-standard car battery that can be exchanged at Battery Swap Stations.

PARK A POLLUTER, TAKE A FREE ELECTRIC   Oaktown pioneers a wave of gasoline- and diesel-engine-free cities in America. Its medieval-looking perimeter wall, topped by a freeway for bicycles and electric cars, is ringed with parking lots for banned, polluting cars which alternate with walled-off areas for free, city-owned electric cars. City cars are recharged by rooftop photo voltaic cells and at public Park 'N' Plug spaces. Citations are issued for "forgetting to plug in." Visitors must leave their unwelcome cars at the edge of town.

LIGHT ENTERTAINMENT RAIL To increase light rail ridership, engineers copy popular Disneyland rides and modify cars and tracks so riders can feel frightening dips, travel into fake mountains, and experience monstrous noises and ghoulish apparitions. Extra transit police are hired after a rash of tunnel muggings.

Distractions
and diversions

The United States in the late 20th century has been compared with the Roman Empire in its final days. Outrageous excess, fascination with new objects and possessions, moral confusion, and a craving for ever more titillating experiences are observed. Americans work hard at inventing systems and products that will distract them.

WHAT TO WATCH FOR:

❑ Campers purchase audiotape machines that play Urban Sounds tapes which help them fall to sleep: Rush Hour Traffic, Neighbors Arguing, Refrigerator Hum and Sounds of Television.

❑ Novel automobile bumpers emit a loud sound when bumped. These foster a new game of 75-mph "freeway auto bumping" and "auto tag."

❑ Football stadiums are created where losing players are "hung" (with hidden straps) from goal posts. Fields are mounded with gullies and hillocks enabling hiding and surprise tackling.

❑ Combat stadiums are built. There are battles between armored teams equipped with lasers, small missiles, and "sound vibration" machines that knock over opponents.

CLIMBING PEOPLE MOVER   Roller coaster design and safety standards are applied to people movers in downtown business and office districts. Each mover accommodates three passengers and glides automatically through or over the surface of buildings.

PUBLIC AMUSEMENTWORKS Funny-looking roads and bridges are designed by public-spirited transit engineers, as visual diversions for tired or anxious travelers.

SKY CAMPING The new generation of campers demands entertainment along with their camping experience. Structures are built for concessions licensed to operate Sky Camping franchises. An overnight fee entitles campers to occupy a platform that they may raise and lower while suspended over a 1,000-foot deep gorge.

CAMPSITE APARTMENTS   Campsite apartments are built at popular recreation sites to relieve sensitive forest areas from the negative impact of soil compaction and ground cover destruction. Sleeping on bare ground is forbidden. The simple, cave-like apartments contain stoves, stairways and bathrooms.

PYRAMID CAMP TOWERS   Like the similar campsite apartments, Pyramid Camp Towers offer a means for enjoying the outdoors while staying in a cave-like room. Each tier has a cement floor, stove, and fence. On the roof, campers enjoy a campfire while singing songs. On starry nights, they sit staring up at the sky.

PRIMITIVE HOTEL   The stressful life of working Americans, who have increasingly less vacation time, leads to a craving for deep engagement with a more natural life. If the family cannot afford to travel to Bali, or to spend time in a thatched hut in Belize, they can check into one of the new so-called primitive hotels. The accommodations are by design extremely rough. A hotel may receive a five-star rating because the primitive experience that is offered is truly uncomfortable. You may be required to grind your own acorns, hunt for your own food, and spend a week without taking a shower. At most primitive hotels, rough animal skin clothing must be worn.

MULTIPLE-CHOICE BEACHES News of a weakening ozone layer prompts new worries over exposure to ultraviolet radiation. Portions of public beaches are set aside for those who believe in covering up in the sun. A line of full-coverage, ultraviolet-blocking swimwear is marketed.

GRAY WATER RECREATION Water sports enthusiasts are informed by government water bureaucrats that they may choose between abandoning their sports, or accepting designated Class II Water Recreation Areas. These are impure, "no guarantees" waters, safe only in full-body wet suits.

WALLCLIMBERS A spectacular innovation for public fun and ostentation is the Wallmaster, a safe but dizzying exercise machine that climbs and descends the exterior of 30-story buildings. Safely harnessed and protected inside "fainting cages," Wallmaster users are advised not to look down. Races are held.

SKYSCRAPER JOGGING RAMPS Downtown skyscrapers are designed with sloped exterior ramps, giving workers an excellent place for hiking, jogging, smoking or sightseeing without fear of being mugged. A guard is stationed at sidewalk level to control ramp access. The ramps serve as fire escapes.

COMMUNAL THEATER SEATING   Cozy seating for groups or families is possible in theaters designed to allow user-defined seating arrangements. Armrests pull down to isolate or connect individuals, couples, and groups. Some group or family members may dislike wiggling or nudging, and pull down their divider. Sterilized rental pillows are available.

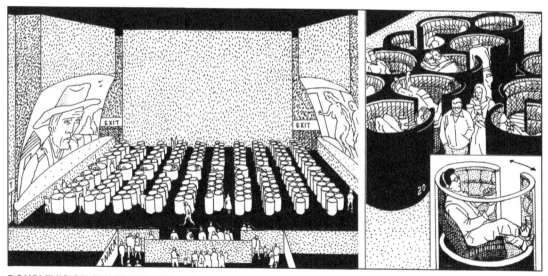

DOUBLEVISION MOVIE THEATER   Theater owners decide to become more competitive to recapture revenues lost to home video rentals and "virtual reality" arcades. An innovation that attracts new theatergoers is DoubleVision, which lets viewers choose between two screens at opposite ends of the theater. They can turn around inside revolving viewing stations, and switch headset channels between screens A and B. The ticket purchase entitles them to stay to watch the movie playing on the opposite wall, if it seems appealing.

ANIMALS CAGED WITH MODERN ART Modern art pieces are placed inside animal cages. The works gain new meaning as animals, lacking human artistic sensibilities, use them for their own purposes. Artists agree to release zoos from responsibility for gnawing, scratching, or droppings damage.

ARTS SUPPORTS Art-in-Public-Places contests engage winning designers to work with highway engineering departments to create amusing sculptural enhancements for freeway support columns.

Tents

ATV

mountain bikes

ALL-IN-ONE RECREATION VEHICLE Rarely was it possible to venture into the woods or back country carrying so many so-called recreational toys, until the All-in-One Recreation Vehicle was created. Its large convertible-style body conceals two mountain bicycles, two tents and an all-terrain vehicle (ATV). This was just what Americans needed!

FUN CARS   Fun cars are 21st-century successors to recreation vehicles. Never intended for rough, environment-damaging back country travel, they appeal to a younger generation that is looking for a sleek sleep out car minus the bloated, motor home look. It features rear entry, a pop-up bed, shower (not shown), and toilet.

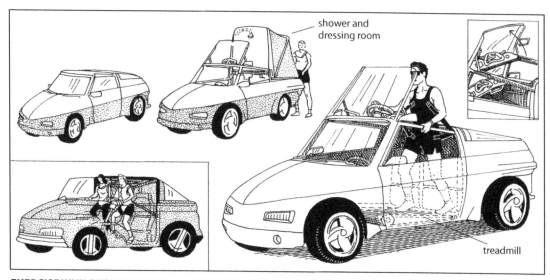

EXERCISE WHILE YOU DRIVE   Convertibles for "exerdriving" are created. Drivers stand up and work out while driving, keeping a grip on hand-operated acceleration and braking controls. Standbelts, which prevent them from being thrown out in a sharp turn or in an accident, must be worn while driving.

RECREATIONAL LAWN MOWERS Unstable rainfall patterns in most areas of the United States make maintaining a bright green lawn illegal during drought season. But wealthy property owners, and Speedy Gardener franchises use mowers either in the noisy Speedski style or the ecologically correct recumbent pedal-powered version.

GOG A marriage of golf and jogging, Gog allows golfers the chance to shed traditional togs for lighter running wear. It gives runners an opportunity to build upper body strength as they enjoy fresh air at a Gog course. Gog club bags are transported on an automated mini-tram that parallels fairways.

TREADAROUNDS Treadarounds are a fun utility that adolescents can use for public cruising and flirting. Affluent young people own souped-up versions, but most rent them at concessions in public parks and promenades. Treadmill and driving wheels work at different speeds simultaneously.

EARLY MODEL SEMI-AUTOMATIC GOLFING CART Before computers are incorporated into golfing machines, there are powered carts with drive belts and hand levers, and adjustments for force, power, and direction of golf swing. The golfer does the thinking, while the machine does doing the work.

SEMI-AUTOMATIC GOLF When golfers feel lazy or have health problems, they use self-propelled semi-automatic golfing machines. A control panel shows split-screen views of the ball and of the terrain ahead, letting golfers program their aim, angle, and force of swing. An on-screen "caddy" offers advice on how to play the hole.

GOLFING CARS A "sports-like" experience is created even as personal exertion is minimized. Golfing Cars offer "auto polo" as golfer-drivers vie for position and make use of computers that assess distance, wind and slope.

BONUS BASEBALL   In large cities noisy, wagering crowds pack Bonus Baseball stadiums to watch this new game of "baseball chance," played on a field resembling a huge pinball machine. Batters try to knock the ball into high-score cups, hoops, holes and troughs. Runners may hide inside tunnels at first and third base.

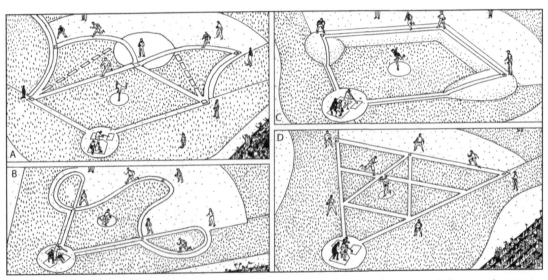

THE DEMISE OF TRADITIONAL BASEBALL There is a movement to create a New Baseball that is no longer tied to formulas and rules established in the late 19th century. A Committee for the New Baseball reconsiders the roles of players. Where, if a ball is hit by a batter, should a player run? Shouldn't the choice of paths mirror the multiplicity of decision paths that characterizes life in the modern world? Stadiums are built that allow "cutting across the field " (A), "running back toward home plate" (B), "running uphill to first base and downhill from third base to home plate" (C), and the dynamic "crisscrossing paths" option (D).

Unique public entertainments

A craving for ever-new spectacles gives rise to a revolution in the museum "business," and sees Urban Planning Departments renamed as Urban Planning and Entertainment Departments. Where public budgets are large enough to justify hefty outlays for novel construction projects, results are often spectacular.

One enjoys the smell of incense and the peculiar calm pervading Judo Baseball stadiums, funded by cities that have a large Asian population. Commissions on the Arts yield to popular demand for "reality rooms" in museums, where humans are viewed in their native habitat.

Special freeway offramps are designed to be so dangerous that drivers consider it a challenge to survive them. These generate revenue for cash-strapped highway departments. The revival of declining downtowns is furthered by the construction of office buildings that showcase formerly-banned trapeze-walking and wall scaling.

ORIENTALIZED BASEBALL   As East rushes to imitate everything Western, the Western institutions are subtly changed. Baseball, already a heavily ritualized game, evolves into new forms. One of the branches features a formal and graceful version of baseball., Judo Baseball. Players sit barefoot in formal posture in the dugouts, practice Tai Chi movements with bats, and bow to the opposing player.

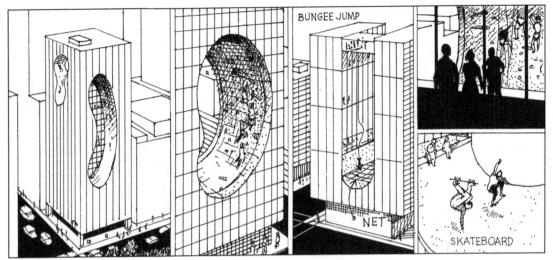

EXTREME SPORTS OFFICE TOWERS   Entertainment increasingly becomes a value, a commodity, that saturates every aspect of the culture. Americans *expect* to be entertained! In central business districts, some tower office structures are constructed to specifically encourage participation in and spectator viewing of extreme sports such as wall climbing, bungee jumping, and exhibition skateboarding.

FREEWAY THRILL EXITS Once state highway departments figure out how to charge users for taking the "thrill exit," there is a construction binge in building exits "for recreational purposes only." They become a big revenue producer. A seriously dangerous loop is a favorite with crowds, who sit in nearby bleachers watching to see if drivers either misjudge a turn or worse–pull back on their speed while traversing a loop, causing their car to fall straight down from the roadway. Drivers are required to pass tests demonstrating above average driving skill in order to use these special exits.

UP CLOSE AND PERSONAL ZOO Within American culture there is an ever-growing taste for more intimate, direct experiences. The trend can be seen in new zoos which bring the animal and the human viewer into closer contact. In some zoos, the viewing stations poke up into the animals' spaces, so that, for example, a lion may be resting a few feet away.

MILITARY ENTERTAINMENT COMPLEX The Public Perception and Recruitment division (PPR) of the U.S. military learned from surveys that a military career is losing its attractiveness among young people. Focus groups are held which deliver an unexpected finding: the military needs to become more entertaining. The result is the creation of parks, the largest ones located in Florida and California, dedicated to a seamless morphing of aspects of military culture with the culture of fun. The parks are popular. Soldiers wear camouflage animal outfits; a tank is made over to look like a coiled rattlesnake.

VIRTUALLY SHOPPING In Videopick supermarkets, customers face cartoon or photographic images of foodstuffs and Sundries, and select items by pressing buttons, levers, or a "virtual reality glove." They query expiration date, cost per ounce, biodegradability, or packaging toxicity before filling their basket.

Services to meet new needs

Public conveniences, services, and spectator sports match the desires and expectations of a particular generation, but not necessarily of those that follow. New public services reflect a tightened economy and a more pronounced layering of social classes.

WHAT TO WATCH FOR:

- ❑ Toxic Dump Identification Clubs offer weekend walks to offensive sites.

- ❑ In Suspendoriums, clients are maintained in drawers in a state of suspended animation, until job and housing opportunities improve.

- ❑ Police persons fly in maneuverable, tiny jet planes that can be stopped and parked quickly. Emergency response times improve.

- ❑ At Planet-Tarry bars, star tenders match up strangers, studying their birth charts for astrological synastry. Clients request "excitement," "sexual tension," or "good friend only" options.

- ❑ As the population ages, Sidewalk Toilets become ubiquitous in downtown areas, and are as common as phone booths of an earlier era.

FREE COMPUTER OR FAX Attempting to reduce dependence on foreign oil, the national government adopts a pilot program of giving a government-maintained, free computer and fax to each household with residents willing to pledge to stop using the mails for sending messages and letters.

INSTANT BOOK PUBLISHING Traditional book publishing and distribution systems compete with "instant" book publishing centers. Using optical disks leased from publishers, the centers offer books printed on back-to-back, one-size-only paper, and "mix and match," or "boring chapter deletion" options.

ERRANDERS All-Transaction Centers have rows of automatic teller stations for such tasks as applying for a job, registering a car, selling a stock, paying a delinquent phone bill, or registering for military draft. Students are hired part-time to do errands for employed professionals, and frequent these centers.

SHOPPING SCOUTS Splits occur in many national organizations, as the gap between rich and poor widens. In the Boy Scouts, Poor Scouts of America build homes for Third Worlders, while Shopping Scouts earn merit badges in Exotic Adventure Sports, Skillfulness With Money, and Wise Suitcase Packing.

PANHANDLING STATIONS In some cities, downtown merchants threaten to move their businesses out of town unless public works departments remodel sidewalks to include panhandling stations. These are dugouts where registered beggars can legally appeal for money to passersby.

TWO-CLASS TRANSIT With almost no national outcry, an anti-egalitarian trend allows public transit systems to separate rich from poor. Two-class planes, trains and buses let persons carrying a MasterPerson card enter guarded quarters where classical music is played and computer lap tops are free.

UPPER-CLASS SOUP KITCHENS   Destitute lawyers, stock brokers and surgeons line up for free meals at discrete, elegantly furnished soup kitchens in affluent neighborhoods. Inside formal dining cafeterias, diners watch a display board that shows precious metals prices, Dow Jones averages, and offers of $100-per-hour temporary work.

ACCOMMODATORS   Accommodators are sited at busy intersections in major cities. In a single location, one can use a phone, go to the bathroom, have an instant photo taken, wait for the bus, buy candy, or be incarcerated in a small holding cell.

PUBLIC LOVE VAN   Mobile mini-motels, dubbed public love vans, park at downtown parking meters. A stay at the motel is charged by the minute, and includes washroom, toilet, shower, and rental movies. Adult reading materials and love toys are sold.

PUBLIC THERAPY BUSES In urban areas, people who are disaffected, alienated or lonely line up to board Public Therapy buses, where they can explain their troubles to a professional psychologist or therapist. In a 15-minute ride, a counselor suggests referrals, summons medical aid, or calls for police.

BUMPER CARTS A chain of entertainment-oriented supermarkets offers opportunities for good-natured, wholesome horseplay during shopping. Electric bumper carts encourage playfulness, though ill-tempered or elderly customers often find the carts jarring or distracting.

INFODINER An Infodiner allows diners to call up a menu on a keyboard, select food preferences, type a seat number, and message a waitress using computer mail. While dining, they may watch a small TV, make phone calls, or call up news briefs or market quotes on the computer. The bill itemizes the services used.

SMOKERS' ENCLOSURES Waiting rooms offer cigarette, cigar and pipe smokers the chance to sit inside an enclosure that drops over their chair. The enclosure provides oxygen, a negative ion air stream and an activated charcoals filter. Each enclosure is thoroughly cleaned weekly.

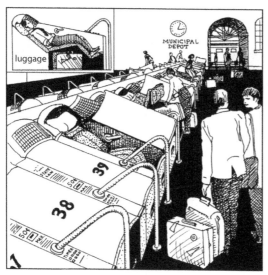

SLUMBER CABINETS Coin-operated Slumber Cabinets with a one-hour limit appear in public train, plane and bus depots. They offer an adjustable reclining seat, a snooze alarm, a lockable hatch, and space for storing carry-on luggage. The units are automatically sanitized after each use.

SIMPLIFIED ROAD SIGN ENGLISH An increasing number of Americans are new immigrants whose native language is not English. They can't expect to know how to pronounce words like plough, cough, through, or tough. To ease confusion, road signs employ phonetic approximations of English.

TRASH DIVIDED Public trash receptacles are redesigned in a way that blatantly acknowledges the national hunger problem.

JUNK MAIL LIBRARY Postage rates for unsolicited mail are hiked after government environmentalists determine that such mail is "not in the public good." Yet many people miss it, so junk mail libraries are created. Advertisers mail batches of their solicitations to these libraries directly, where they are cataloged and displayed.

POWER WORSHIP   Two health-oriented churches are founded. One is the Healthy Me Sanctuary, which offers hushed, solemn cubicles for performing the Twelve Stations of Self-Examination (Pap Smear, Urine Sample, etc.). The object of worship is Yourself. Lectures focus on how to avoid physical and nervous collapse. Another church, Power Worship, has a joyful, sweaty, evangelical atmosphere. Vocal prayer, led by a physically-fit prayer leader, is timed to match the pace of "stair-climbing" exercise machine routines. Worshippers commonly leave group prayer sessions limp with emotional and physical exhaustion.

BILLBOARD HONESTY   The New Honesty, as it is popularly called, becomes a fad for pushing unpleasant things into the open. Truth-In-Advertising laws are expanded to include all public signage, including billboards. Health purists convince lawmakers to require a skull-and-crossbones label on sugar.

DO-IT-YOURSELF PLAZA   The do-it-yourself shop trend spreads from copy-it-yourself or frame-your-own-picture centers to public places where trained assistants stand by while you use a rental blowtorch or a surgery knife. Americans enjoy de-mystifying specialty professions.

DRIVE-TO RESTAURANT The opposite of a drive-in restaurant, the truck-mounted Drive-to Restaurant brings the dining experience to a different neighborhood each night. It advertises its future locations in advance. Phone reservations are taken. Often, residents living nearby leave their car at home and enjoy walking to the cafe.

UNIVERSAL CAR COMPANY Planned auto design obsolescence is decried by consumer groups. Universal Car Company offers a "5-year, no changes" guarantee. Unicar stations advertise "24-hour mechanics and parts availability" and "Emergency Waiting Rooms."

ON-RAMP SERVICES Bankrupt state transportation departments, still shying from taking hard steps necessary to snap the collective automobile addiction, resort to cute inducements like car wash onramps and "fun" offramps to help fund freeway maintenance and construction.

DRIVE-UP STORE Hundreds of individual car trips to buy cigarettes, toilet paper, or diapers are saved when drive-up stores make scheduled stops along bus routes. The buses stop long enough for lined-up shoppers to use a customers-only bathroom, buy soft drinks, auto steering fluid, popcorn, potato chips or instant coffee. The opposite of drive-in stores, they also stock items for home business entrepreneurs, such as computer paper, floppy disks, and typing ribbons. They also offer fax and copy services. A bell announces when five minutes remain for making selections before the store moves on to its next stop.

EMERGENCY WAYS Fire trucks, police cars, ambulances, and toxic spill cleanup vehicles are redesigned to allow for exclusive access to elevated emergency roadbeds, monorails or trams, for faster response in emergencies.

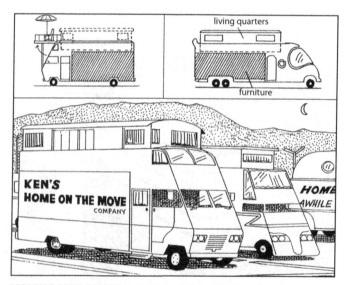

MOVING VAN HOME Restless job seekers and temporary or reassigned employees rent moving van homes when they must move from city to city. In an unfamiliar town, they can come home to modest living quarters above a load of their own furniture.

Taking care of kids and elders

A nation bent on amusing itself and catering to selfish and personal needs has trouble figuring out how to deal with its less fit, less capable, less muscular, less mentally developed children and elders. It is not deemed a good idea to simply get rid of them! But what to do with them, when the purpose of life increasingly is believed to be hasty and full-speed-ahead self-fulfillment?

Some states decide that children are too costly to maintain, generally speaking, when considering their low output and minimal usefulness. There are school districts, for example, that discover how to stop building schools entirely, when the school bus and the classroom are designed as a single unit.

Finding ways to deal with the growing elderly population is another problem. One moderately successful solution is to house them, along with their grandchildren, at their children's workplace.

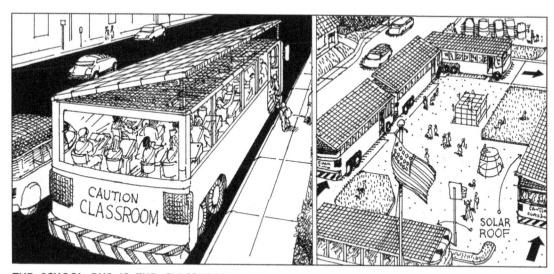

THE SCHOOL BUS IS THE CLASSROOM The blatantly inefficient system of sending children to school in classroom-sized buses, only to deliver them to their "real" classrooms, eventually becomes obsolete. It dawns on some school districts that a slightly wider and more neatly appointed school bus, with modern, fold-down desks, can serve as both bus and school.

DAY CARE FOR INFANTS AND SENIORS Companies experience employee problems caused by demands and pulls of family life, as these may "interfere" with work productivity. To address this growing problem at a time when young workers increasingly "live" at work, offices are redesigned to incorporate child care and seniors care facilities that are visible from the office floor. The experiment is only partially successful. The natural inclination to pay attention to one's child, who may have a skinned knee, or to a grandparent who is suffering from fainting spells, is found to scatter the attention of an employee whose relatives are nearby, behind glass.

COMPUTER CLASS FOR THE INFIRM Old folks do, indeed, become old and infirm as they always have. But elders now living in America in many cases possess a growing taste for learning and for using the computer. A trend emerges where one of the "activities" for elders is using and learning computer skills.

Rebellion and dying cities

While an ever-narrowing slice of the U.S. population enjoys historically unprecedented wealth and access to the best of everything, many less wealthy members of the population watch in frustration as government budgets at all levels are slashed. Shrinking budgets result in school and park closures and in a serious decline in policing, regulation enforcement, and national infrastructure maintenance. Parks are abandoned and allowed to return to a "natural" state, which then become places of refuge for criminals. Fires blaze out of control in national forests in the West, and there are no budgets for replanting. Some urban areas become so dangerous that civic authorities declare the areas to be officially out of control. Entering such a neighborhood, one signs a release exempting the government from liability in case of harm or death. As a mood of rebellion grows, walled-off reservations are set aside for non-conformists. If you are willing to step outside the protections of U.S. law, you may choose to live there.

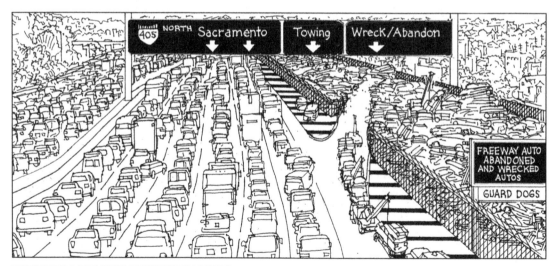

FREEWAY LANES BECOME WRECKING YARD
In some urban areas freeway traffic is stalled for most of the day. Drivers, in a fit of rage, may smash their car into the sidewall or into other cars, or abandon it. Three lanes are converted into a permanent, miles-long wrecking yard.

URBAN PERSONAL RISK ZONE Dangerous neighborhoods are declared Personal Risk Zones. Drivers may purchase additional life insurance at entry gates, and may choose to have Car Armor–made of soft, loose-fitting Kevlar and bulletproof plastic for windows–attached to their car.

BUILDING REGULATION-FREE ZONE City building departments give up on urban areas that have become uncontrollable. Illegal immigration spawns shack cities that rival districts in Buenos Aires. Districts that are declared Regulation Unsustainable Inspection Negative (RUIN) are walled-off in order to contain the blight.

RESERVATIONS FOR NON-CONFORMISTS As the nation becomes less tolerant of eccentric thinkers and non-conformists, reservations are set aside for these so-called "non-assimilables." They write their own laws and police themselves.

BURNED FOREST CAMPGROUNDS The charge to stay overnight at a burned out campsite is reduced due to the lower quality of the camping experience. These sites are increasingly common in the West. Campers must wear special clothes, including gloves and overshoes, that may become smeared with charcoal.

Unabashed praise, heartless bashing

The ideas and artwork in the first edition of *Public Therapy Buses* stimulated a range of comments both from supportive friends, authors and futurists, and from unhappy, ill-tempered literalists:

GENERALLY POSITIVE COMMENTS

Steven Johnson has far more in common with Buckminster Fuller than the cluttered, cheerfully vulgar Robert Crumb. The artists Johnson reminds me of are *The New Yorker*'s Bruce McCall, who has come up with some wild inventions of his own, and Guy Billout, who does those wonderfully surreal full-page illustrations for The Atlantic Monthly. I've been fans of their work for years, but I'd never heard of Steven Johnson.

> –T. Quinn, online comment, 2009

I think the PEDALTRAIN is the best idea of them all!! I think he should find some grant money and build a prototype.

> –Galit, online comment, 2009

I was given a copy of *Public Therapy Buses* for my birthday when I was 12, in 1992. Probably affected me in ways I'm not aware of, esp. because despite being technically "cartoons," it isn't intended for kids at all. One aspect of the books that the writer of this piece doesn't give much space to is how dark his vision of America is.

> –Ezra, online comment, 2009

It's just uncanny how many of the things pictured humorously in this 1991 book have essentially come into existence and become part of our lives in 2010. Who IS this guy??

> –Handpicked Books, San Francisco, 2010

The product of a wonderfully diseased mind.

> –Nutjob, online comment, 2009

Steven Johnson is the most under-known artist/inventor/humorist in the world. He is also the best. I would love to see him gain a wider audience.

> –Peter Parsons, 2009

His work should be a textbook for elementary school students!

> –Robert Fritz, online comment

I remember his having this wonderful deadpan humor in (journalism) class, and he certainly has carried that into his art...His drawings are seemingly understated, but they have tremendous force–at the same time they are funny. It's a rare combination to have this kind of social power and to be funny, not grim about it.

> –Alan Temko, author, U.C. Berkeley professor of journalism, environmental critic for San Francisco Chronicle, 1991

Steven M. Johnson has seen the future and it's weird...There is social commentary in *Public Therapy Buses.* Mr. Johnson zeros in on a current trend and pushes it–from here to absurdity.

> –Thomas D. Sullivan, Washington Times, 1991

You start looking at these drawings and start to ponder just what is going on here, and you begin to think about the possibilities of the future and how we're going to manage the future that Steve Johnson envisions.

> –Edward Cornish, President of the World Future Society, 1992

Ideas (both ingenious and totally goofy), drastic extremes, nasty innuendos, laughs-up-the-sleeve, future schlock and subtle horror (you know at least some are gonna happen no matter what) make up this collection of snidely captioned drawings of proposed technology. Nifty, nasty, and occasionally hysterically funny.

> –J. Baldwin, Whole Earth Review, 1992

His art falls somewhere among cartoons, blueprints and flights of fancy, but the common theme is his interest in the future and ingenuity in design.

> –Brooke Thomas, Palo Alto Weekly, 2007

I look forward to Mr. Johnson's whimsical and well thought out illustrations. I consider them "neat."

> –xadrian, online comment, 2011

Many of his musings are simply whimsical, existing primarily as a source of inspiration or delight. Others tackle very real issues, from environmentalism to alternative transportation to homelessness.

> –Allison Arieff, columnist, The New York Times, 2009

Public Therapy Buses is mind popping, laugh out loud, look at what life could be like if a pack of insane industrial designers were allowed to rework just about everything. This 1991 peek into an alternate universe is a hilarious *tour de force* of unfettered design and vision where all the trains are pedal powered, and your cubicle at work (sadly) converts into your tiny home at night. Brilliant!!
—*Javin Pierce, CEO and founder, Pierce Instruments Inc., 2013*

REMARKS BY DETRACTORS AND "TROLLS"

But can he make any of the things he draws? An inventor produces real things that work in the real world, and don't just look nice on paper.
—*koeppelkoeppel, online comment, 2009*

I have yet to see an idea from this artist that I like. The ideas are often impractical and sometimes dangerous (and sometimes are already out there?).
—*Jimbo, online comment, 2011*

This crap has got to go. It's stupid and pointless beyond comprehension. Almost all the designs are unwieldy and pointless (except for that full-mouth tooth-brushing gizmo).
—*Another David, online comment, 2011*

I am eagerly awaiting another rumored invention of Steven M. Johnson. It's a cup shaped object for holding, transporting, and drinking coffee out of. I think he tentatively was going to call it a "coffee cup"
—*Joe Citizen, online comment, 2010*

Thanks

Persons thanked in the First Edition:
John and Pam Blanpied, Jon Buller, Ed Canale, Jim Fitzgerald, Ken Horton, Alex S. Johnson, Beatrice Johnson, Leonard Koren, Alex Kuczynski, Hatley Mason, Ann Myren, Allen Pierlioni, Pamela Pasti, and Rita Sullenberger.

Others who have encouraged me in my work along the way since 1991: Allison Arieff, Mark Ashcraft, Sheldon Carpenter, Jim Carr, Dirk Dieter, Paul Duginski, Jim and Sondra Erickson, Leonard Foote, Peter Haugen, Kikuo Hayashi, Steve Heller, Sidney Magee, Tim McCormick, Ed Murrieta, Peter Parsons, Javin Pierce, Michael and Ieva Portnoy, Alex Santoso, Lynne Shaw, Norm Sperling, and Thomas Sullivan.
Special thanks for help with design questions: Sheldon Carpenter, Michael Shallow, and Karen Skelton.

The author

Steven M. Johnson was born in 1938 in San Rafael, California. He was educated at Yale University and the University of California at Berkeley. His whimsical product concepts first appeared in *The Sierra Club Bulletin* in 1973 and have since been published in numerous magazines including *Harper's, Road & Track, The Futurist, New Age Journal, Whole Earth Review, Nexus, Funny Times, Tur & Retur* (Sweden), *Box* (Japan), and *Brutus* (Japan). Since 2009 his work has appeared online in *Bloomberg Businessweek, Esquire, The New York Times, The Atlantic, Good, FastCompany, Design Mind, Esquire* and *Txchnologist* as well as on other sites. From 1989 to 1995, his work appeared weekly in *The Sacramento Bee* as "A Step Ahead." It was also distributed from 1992-1995 by Carmen Syndicate as "Sightings." His first book, published in 1984, was *What The World Needs Now*. A second and third edition of the book have been published. In 2012, *Have Fun Inventing* was published. This book is the third edition of *Public Therapy Buses*, first published in 1991. A second edition was published in 2013.

He lives in Northern California with his wife, Beatrice. His son, Alex S. Johnson is an author and editor who also lives in California.

Made in the USA
Monee, IL
03 June 2020